JN303198

語彙力アップの秘密

リーディングに効く!

The "Secrets" To Better English Vocabulary

Gaburiel David Munoz
＋
水嶋いづみ 著

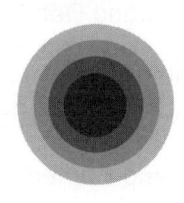

研究社

Contents

Introduction 1

Chapter 1 About Vocabulary 3
Chapter 2 Using a Dictionary 9
Chapter 3 Taking Words Apart 15
Chapter 4 Prefixes 20
Chapter 5 The Greeks and Latins 29
Chapter 6 Roots 36
Chapter 7 The Source of Origin 44
Chapter 8 Suffixes 50
Chapter 9 More Suffixes 57
Chapter 10 Suffixes, Parts of Speech, and Spelling 64
Chapter 11 Homonyms 70
Chapter 12 Compounding Words 78
Chapter 13 Synonyms, Antonyms, and Clipped Words 84
Chapter 14 Articles 91
Chapter 15 Knowledge is Reading 98
Chapter 16 The Reading Process 104
Chapter 17 Identifying Topics, Main Ideas, and Supporting Details 109
Chapter 18 Making Inferences and Drawing Conclusions 114
Chapter 19 Reading and Remembering! 121
Chapter 20 Concentrating and Remembering 129
Chapter 21 English Spelling Rules 135
Chapter 22 Exceptions to the Rules 144
Chapter 23 Conclusion 151

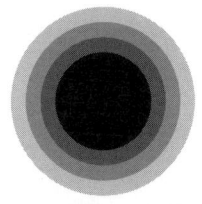
Introduction
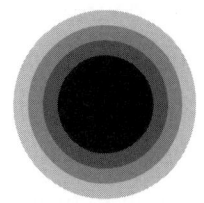

Over the years, I have heard ESL students explain why they have troubles understanding and speaking English. "I don't have enough words" is the most common explanation, although some native speakers
5 call it an excuse.

ESL English as a Second Language 第二言語としての英語

I've also heard a lot of native speakers teaching in conversation schools and even in universities complain that the students are lazy and not motivated. I must say in over twenty years of ESL teaching, I have
10 never come across a lazy or unmotivated student. What I have come across are students who have problems dealing with the language because they have not been properly taught how to read, how to figure out the meaning of unknown English words, or how to
15 learn those words. They have been taught to memorize them, but not how to learn them, they have been taught to look in a dictionary but not to understand what they are seeing, just to get the translation in their mother tongue.

motivated やる気のある

20 While conversation schools say they are interested in teaching you how to speak English, they're really interested in only making money. How can you speak, if you do not know or understand the words that you should use to speak?

25 Universities sell you a textbook, put you in an Eng-

Introduction

lish course, and hope that you come out of the classroom understanding and speaking English. Nobody is saying or thinking "Hey, let's teach them the 'secrets' they need to learn for expanding their vocabulary, which in turn leads to better understanding what they read, and better scores on tests like the TOEIC and TOEFL, and finally better conversations in English."

This is why I worked on writing this book; to help you and all those countless students who "do not have enough words." The secrets actually are very easy to learn. If you want to learn the words to better English vocabulary, which in turn should lead you and other students into becoming better writers and speakers of the English language, do not put this book down.

Whether you are a man, woman, high school, or university student, beginner, intermediate or advanced level, this book (and its "secrets") is for you. Enjoy!

Gabriel David Munoz

countless 無数の

better ～を向上させる

Chapter 1
About Vocabulary

ある程度の長さの英文をきちんと理解するためには、文法の知識はもちろん必要ですが、最終的には単語をどれだけ知っているかが鍵となります。では語彙力をつけるにはどうしたらよいのでしょうか？ そのための"秘密"を授けようというのが本書です。第4章以降で「語彙力アップの秘密」をお伝えしていきますが、その前に本章で単語の重要性を改めて確認しておきましょう。

The Value of Improving Vocabulary

There are five "secrets" in this book, which will help you to improve your vocabulary. They are the type of "secrets" that native English speakers learn at an early age and reinforce throughout their school years. You as an "English as a Second Language" student need to learn these "secrets" and learn how to use them when you come across new words. If you have troubles understanding any of the words you will see and read, do not be afraid to use a dictionary. I have tried to use the easiest words possible to explain, whenever I could.

Vocabulary building takes time and nonstop effort. Your vocabulary can and should be a likeness of you. Your vocabulary is you! And like you, your vocabulary should be alive. It should change and grow to meet your needs.

likeness 類似、肖像、似姿

Chapter 1

The Goal of Vocabulary

Words are great subjects to look into. When you become a student of words, and take pleasure in finding out about word families, and come to know how you can make words work for you, you are more likely to stop when you come across an unfamiliar word and think about its meaning. If you do this, you will become a master of words and your vocabulary will grow.

Why Vocabulary Training Is Important

* Vocabulary is a necessary part of understanding reading. If you don't know enough words, you are going to have trouble understanding what you read. A lone unknown word may not stop you, but if there are too many words you don't know, understanding will suffer.

* Vocabulary is a major part of almost every test, including TOEIC, TOEFL, Eiken, and college entrance exams. Vocabulary is a main point of both one's learning and one's ability to learn. The more words you know, then, the better you are going to do on such important tests.

* Research has shown that students with strong vocabularies are more successful in school and work and that a good vocabulary is a powerful reason for people who enjoy successful careers in life. Words are the tools not just of better reading, but of better writing, speaking, listening, and thinking as well. The more words you have at your control, the more suc-

---

student of words　ことばを学ぶ者
word family　①語幹とその活用形および派生形を含めた単語のグループ　②韻を踏んでいる単語のグループ

cessful your communications can be, and the more impact you can have on the people around you.

*In today's world, a good vocabulary counts more than ever. Many jobs offer English services or deal with English information, and the skills of reading, writing, listening, and speaking are important. The keys to strength and victory in the English place of work are the skills to communicate well and learn quickly. A solid vocabulary is necessary for both of these skills.

During your school years, new English words will be coming into your mind. Many of them are the keys to ideas and information that will be new to you. When students have trouble in a test or course, the trouble can often be traced down back to their poor understanding of expressions that are necessary to the understanding of subject matter. Then there are also words which may not exactly be new to you, but which have certain meanings inside the background of an individual course and as a result must be learned as if they were new words.

For a student, a large, wide-ranging vocabulary is a necessary tool for coming to terms with original ideas and facts. Words are the tools of communication, learning, and thinking, and a student with a too small vocabulary cannot perform successfully and usefully.

The Origin of Words

Words, like facts, are difficult to remember out of context. Remembering is greatly made possible,

count 重要である、価値がある

English place of work = workplace where English is used

come to terms with X
X に慣れる、折り合いがつく

Chapter 1

when you have an amount of information with which to connect either a word or a fact. For words, interesting beginning or histories will help provide a context. For example, a hippopotamus is a "river horse," from
5 the Greek *hippos* meaning "horse," and *potamus*, meaning "river."

Indiana is called the Hoosier state, and its people Hoosiers. Why? In the early days, the pioneers were bad-tempered in manner; when someone knocked at
10 the front door, a pioneer's voice would often roar, "Who's yere?"

If you were offered a Hobson's choice, would you know what was meant? Thomas Hobson owned a livery stable (stable that rents out horses) in seven-
15 teenth-century England. He loved his horses, and to prevent any one horse from being worked too much, he hired them out in turn, beginning with stall number one. Customers had to take the horses they were given. Thus Hobson's choice means no choice at all.

20 Etymology is the study of the origins of words. The English language is living and growing. Although many of our words have been part of our language for many years, new words are added all the time. Following are different ways our language is shaped.

25 • From Foreign Words—English, in many cases, has been on average increased by adding foreign words into it. Most of our language has very old Anglo-Saxon (member of Germanic people) or Latin (language of the old Roman Empire) origins. Other

---

hippopotamus　カバ

bad-tempered　機嫌の悪い、気難しい
roar　大声でわめく、うなり声を上げる

stable　馬小屋

hire out　賃貸しする
stall　馬房

languages have also added to our vocabularies.

- Additions through Technology & Products—Our words often show current interests, styles, and new ideas or methods. One of the latest contributors to our language has been computer technology, which has created words such as *bytes*, *monitor*, *e-mail*, *file sharing*, *downloading*, and *disk*.

- Another way new words come into our language is through the creation of products. Some examples include: *Kleenex*, *Walkman*, *Scotch tape*, *Xerox*, *iPod* and *Coca-Cola*.

- People's Names—sometimes when a person invents or introduces something, that thing becomes associated with the person's name. The person, through time, is forgotten while the name lives on in our language. Examples include:

    mesmerize— F. A. Mesmer, an Austrian doctor and hypnotist.
    sideburns— an American English variation of burnsides. Ambrose E. Burnside was a Northern Army general in the American Civil War.

mesmerize 催眠術をかける、魅惑する

sideburns 頬ひげ、もみあげ

army general 陸軍大将

civil war 内戦、[米] 南北戦争 (1861–65)

- Words from Letters—The initials for the names of things may actually come to replace the names. The initials become the words that represent the thing, idea, or group. The following are examples of words that have developed from initials.

Chapter 1

TV	Television	
COD	Cash On Delivery	cash on delivery　代金引換払い、着払い
N.A.T.O	North Atlantic Treaty Organization	

Exercise

Answer the questions in complete sentences.

1. What is a necessary part of understanding reading?
2. What is vocabulary a main point of?
3. What has research shown?
4. What counts more than ever in today's world?
5. Where did words come from?

Chapter 2
Using a Dictionary

わからない単語に出会ったとき、英和辞典で英単語の「日本語訳」を調べただけで満足してしまっていませんか。辞書に書かれている日本語訳のどれかを適当に当てはめてすっと理解できる英文ばかりであればいいのですが、どの日本語訳で試しても意味がすっきり通らなかったり、あまりにも多くの日本語訳があって、どれを当てはめればいいのか途方に暮れてしまったりすることもあるのではないでしょうか。本章でより効果的な辞書の使い方を学び、辞書を「読む」楽しさをぜひ味わってください。

Using a Good English Dictionary

Many students cheat themselves when they use their mother language-English dictionaries. When they come up on a word they do not know, most of them
5 think all they need is the word's meaning in their mother tongue. They get the English word in their language and then close the dictionary and that is not good because they are only learning the translation into their mother language and not the meaning of the
10 word in English.

One of the best ways to learn new words is to keep a good English dictionary close at hand and use it. Sometimes, you can get some idea of the meaning of a new word from its **context**—how it is used in your
15 reading material. Use context when you can, but be aware that it has its limitations. Using context has the following three limits:

Chapter 2

1. Context provides only the meaning that fits that particular situation.
2. You often end up with a **synonym** (word meaning the same as another), which is not the same as a **definition** (meaning).
3. When you have to **infer** (guess), the meaning of a word, you can be slightly or very wrong.

Your safest bet is to stay away from all the guesswork and go straight to your dictionary. As you study, check in your dictionary whenever you come to a word that you don't know exactly. Find the exact meaning you need; then go back to your textbook and reread the paragraph, with the meaning substituted for the word. Then write the unknown word in a notebook. Later, go back to the dictionary and examine it. Write its meanings in the notebook, and look through and study it at times when you are free.

Get yourself a pocket English dictionary, and always carry it with you. Its definitions will be brief, mainly of synonyms, but its value is in its ability to start an interest in words, as well as increase your vocabulary. Of course, a pocket English dictionary is no substitute for a bigger, desk-size English dictionary; but as a portable learning tool, the pocket dictionary is well worth it.

For careful word study, however, there is no substitute for a full-length dictionary. Find the full-length dictionaries in your library or English self-study center and use them in addition to your own abridged desk dictionary. A full-length dictionary gives more

---

(the) safest bet　最も安全な方法・策
guesswork　当て推量

substitute A for B　Bの代わりにAを使う

substitute　代用品

definitions, more about the beginning of words, and more on the use of those words.

Understanding a Dictionary's Entry

A normal dictionary **entry** (piece of written information) includes these parts:

1. The word or phrase broken into **syllables** (unit of spoken language).
2. The word or phrase with the pronunciation indicated through the use of accent mark/symbols that point out the vowel sounds such as a long vowel or a vowel affected by other sounds; a mark called the **schwa** which tells you that the vowel is in a no-accent syllable of the word.
3. The part or parts of speech the word functions as, for example, a noun (n.), verb (v.), adjective (adj.), or adverb (adv.).
4. Related forms of the word, such as the plural form of nouns and the past tense of verbs.
5. The definition or definitions of the word or phrase. Generally dictionaries group the definitions according to a word's use as a noun, verb, adjective, and/or adverb.
6. The origin, or history, of the word or words, such as from the Latin, Old French, Middle English, Hebrew, and/or the name of a person. Some dictionaries use the symbol < to mean "came from." For example, the origin of the word *flank* is given as "< Old French *flanc* < Germanic." This tells us that *flank* came from the Old French word *flanc*. The French word in

syllable 音節

Middle English 中(期)英語 (11〜15世紀頃の英語。この時期に大量のフランス語が流入した)
Hebrew ヘブライ語

flank わき腹、(競技場の) サイド、側面 (に位置する)

turn, came from the German language. Some dictionaries use abbreviations to tell you where the item came from: OE for Old English, L for Latin, and so forth.

abbreviation 省略形、略語、略記

5 **Understanding a dictionary entry using the following steps:**
- Pronounce the word in syllables using the accent marks as a guide.
- Note the part or parts of speech of the word and any related words.
10 • Read the definitions.
- Check the origin of the word reference to see if you can find bits and pieces of the meaning of the first word in the meaning of the entry.
- Use the word in a sentence that has a clue in it as to
15 the meaning of the word.

bits and pieces こまごまとした物

clue 手がかり

Spelling and the Dictionary

One of the most useful sources of spelling information is a dictionary.

Main Entry information
20 • **Syllable divisions**—when a word contains more than one syllable, it is entered in the dictionary with a small space between each syllable.
- **Hyphenation**—some words are always spelled with a hyphen (dash or line, showing that the word
25   must be divided). The dictionary entry will show this hyphen, if there is one.
- **Word divisions**—some dictionary entries are made up of two words. A two-word entry will usually have a large space between the two words.

- **Capitalization**—if a word is usually spelled with a capital, its entry will also be spelled with a capital. If a word has two uses but only one of them is capitalized, the dictionary may list them under two entries—for example, God (the Almighty) and god (any supernatural being that is worshipped).

Outside the Main Entry

Sometimes a dictionary can provide help in spelling certain kinds of words that may not be listed as main entries. These are special grammatical forms or suffixed forms. Here are some:

- **Comparative and Superlative forms of adjectives**—for examples, the two words *crazier* and *craziest*, which are formed from *crazy*.
- **Verb Forms**—for example, the words *crackled* and *crackling*, which are formed from the verb *crackle*.
- **Suffixed Forms**—for example, the adverb *craftily* and the noun *craftiness*, which are formed from the adjective *crafty*.
- **Noun Forms**—for example, the words *babies*, which is formed from *baby*.

The above example words are not always main entry words, although the words from which they are formed are main entries. They are often listed within the entry of the word from which they are formed. Not all possible grammatical or suffixed forms are listed after the main entry. Those that are listed are often those that involve spelling problems.

---

almighty　全能の神、全能者
supernatural being　超自然的存在
worship　崇拝する、礼拝する

Other Spellings

As you are surely aware, many words have more than one spelling. When a word has two common spellings, the dictionary will often include them both. Here are some of the main ways they may be listed:

- The most common spelling will be a main entry, with a full definition after it.
- Different, less common spellings are sometimes listed in the body of the main entry, either near the beginning or at the end. These other spellings may follow the words *or,* or *also*.
- The less common spelling may also have an entry of its own. It will not have a full definition after it, however.

Exercise

Answer true or false.

1. There is no need to use a dictionary when you do not know a word.
2. All you need to learn a word is to memorize it.
3. When using a dictionary you should pronounce the word in *syllables* using the accent marks as a guide.
4. Read the definitions.
5. Many words have only one spelling.

Chapter 3
Taking Words Apart

日本語の熟語が複数の漢字から成り立っており、それぞれの漢字の意味を組み合わせれば熟語全体の意味がなんとなくわかるように、英単語の多くも単語を構成しているパーツの意味を足し算していくことによって意味を推測することができます。英単語を構成するパーツとして接頭辞、語根、接尾辞があります。本章では、これらのパーツにどんな働きがあるのか、そしてどのように組み合わさって単語が出来上がっていくのかを学びます。

"The Secret of Words"

The Greeks and Romans came up with a plan for making words by putting together smaller word parts. They used three types of word parts: **prefixes**, **suffixes**, and **roots**. *Pre-* means "before," and so it makes sense that a prefix comes before the main part of a word. *Suf-* means "after," and so a suffix comes at the end of a word. A root is the main part of a word, and usually comes in the middle. Many English words are made up of at least one root, and many have one or more prefixes and suffixes. Prefixes and suffixes are known as **affixes** (meaning "added to words").

prefix 接頭辞
suffix 接尾辞
root 語根

affix 接辞

Word parts play an important part in the total meaning of a word. Each part has its own meaning. The meaning of an unknown word often is a mixture of its parts.

Word parts give the important meanings. Studying the parts of words can tell you many things. The **base**

Chapter 3

of a word gives you an overall meaning for the unknown word. Affixes affect the base's meaning. Some affixes give general meanings. Others identify the subject area of the unknown word. Affixes also
[5] help reveal the **part of speech** (verb, noun, adjective, adverb, etc.) of the unknown word.

base 語基

reveal 明らかにする

- *Prefixes and suffixes change or refine a word's meaning*. For example the word *audible* means "able to be heard." However, add the prefix *in-* and
[10] the word becomes *inaudible,* which means "unable to be heard."
- *A word can contain more than one root*. For example, *matrilineal* contains the root *matri* (mother) and *lineal* (line). *Matrilineal* therefore,
[15] means "determining origin through the female line."

matrilineal 母系の、母方の

Adding Prefixes and Suffixes to Roots

A **prefix** is a letter or group of letters added to the front of a word that changes the meaning of the word.
[20] A suffix does the same thing at the end of a word. In this section you are given a map to read the order of roots, prefixes, and suffixes.

Table 3–1 Putting Prefixes, Roots and Suffixes Together		
Prefix + Root + Suffix	**= Word**	**Definition**
ab + duct + ed	= abducted	kidnapped
de + ter + ent	= deterrent	obstacle
dis + pell + ed	= dispelled	scattered
im + peril + ed	= imperiled	put in danger

in + cred + ible	=	incredible		beyond belief
re + puls + ion	=	repulsion		strong dislike
re + tract + able	=	retractable		move something back inside

Recognizing Word Roots and Prefixes

While using the dictionary is a wonderful way to increase your vocabulary one word at a time, if you would like to learn whole groups of words at one time, you should get to know the most common roots and prefixes in English.

Though knowing the meanings of prefixes and roots can unlock the meanings of unfamiliar words, this knowledge should add to, not replace, your dictionary use. Over the years, many prefixes have changed in both meaning and spelling. While some prefixes have a single unchanging meaning, most prefixes have more than one meaning each.

For example, the prefix *de-* means "of" or "from"; yet the dictionary lists four different meanings for it. So learn as many of the common prefixes and roots as you can, but learn them for a better and more clear-cut understanding of words you already know and words that you have yet to look up in the dictionary.

Common Prefixes

- *de-* has various meanings in the words that are formed, including: from, away from, off; down; wholly, entirely, utterly, complete; reverse the action of; undo; the negation or reversal of the notion expressed in the primary word.

- *re-* means "back, backward, again" as in *reconsider* (consider again) or *reconnect* (connect again). It can also mean "back" as in *recall* (call back).
- *in-* changes or is assimilated to *il-* before *l* (*illuminate*); to *im-* before *b* (*imbibe*), before *m* (*immediate*), and before *p* (*implant*); and to *ir-* before *r* (*irrigate*). In all its forms *in-* can mean "not" (*illiterate, immodest*) or some form of "in": "within" (*inhabit, inherit*), "put into" (*enthrone*), "provide with" (*empower*), and "surround" (*envelope*).
- *pre-* means "before [both in time and place]" (*preteen* = before 13 years old; *prenatal* = taking place prior to birth) or "in front of" (*precede* = go in front of).

illiterate 読み書きのできない
immodest 慎みのない、うぬぼれた
enthrone ～を王位に就かせる
empower ～に権利・力を与える

Sometimes it is hard to decide whether you should **hyphenate** (to separate or join words or parts of words using a **hyphen**) these prefixes. Use a hyphen in the following situations.

a. When not hyphenating may cause confusion about the words meaning: *re-creation* (a second creation) against *recreation* (having fun), or *re-form* (to form again) against *reform* (to change from bad to good)
b. When the word following the prefix repeats the letters in the prefix (*re-recover,* for example)
c. When the second element is a proper noun or starts with a capital letter (such as *un-American* and *pre-Historic* or *pre-Christianity*)

Chapter 3

Exercise

Answer true or false.

1. The British came up with a system for creating words.
2. Prefixes and suffixes do change or improve a word's meaning.
3. A word can't contain more than one root.
4. A prefix is a group of letters added to the back of a word.
5. A suffix is added at the front of a word.
6. Word parts do play an important part in the total meaning of a word.
7. Words parts give the important meanings.
8. Studying the parts of words do not tell you anything.
9. The front of a word gives you an overall meaning for the word.
10. *Affixes* help show the *part of speech* of a word.

Chapter 4
Prefixes

英単語が接頭辞や語根や接尾辞で成り立っていることを前章で学びました。本章はそのうちの接頭辞を詳しく見ていきます。接頭辞は元の単語の意味を、接尾辞は元の単語の品詞を変えてしまうものですから、接頭辞や接尾辞の意味を知っているか知っていないかによって英文の理解度が大きく違ってきます。「語彙力アップの秘密」その1はこの接頭辞の知識を指します。接頭辞の意味を知ることで、すでに知っている単語もその成り立ちがはっきりと見えるようになり、本質的な意味がつかめるようになるでしょう。

Here Is Secret #1
re-

Re- is added to almost any verb or its derivative (a word that is formed from another word; for example, "quickly" from "quick" or "electricity" from "electric"), meaning: a) *once more, afresh, anew* (*readjust, renumber*), b) *back* meaning return to a previous state (*reassemble, reverse*). A hyphen is normally used when the word begins with *e* (*re-enact*), or to distinguish the compound from a more familiar one-word form (*re-form*=form again).

Table 4–1   re-Words

Word	Definition
reclaim	act of recalling, or state of being recalled, to a proper conduct
reduction	act or process of bringing something down in extent, amount, or degree; diminish
reflect	to cast back (light, heat, sound, etc.) from a surface: "The mirror reflected the light onto the wall"

Chapter 4

rejuvenate	to restore something to its condition when it was new, or to make it more vigorous, dynamic, and effective
reminisce	to talk or to write about events remembered from the past
reset	to set again
remain	to stay back
renumber	to put in a new order, count or label again
replace	to find a substitute for someone or something that has gone
resident	a person who resides or dwells in a place
rewire	to wire again

de-

De- has various meanings in the words that are formed, including: from, away from, off; down; wholly, entirely, utterly, complete; reverse the action
5 of; undo; the negation or reversal of the notion expressed in the primary word: a) down, away (*descend, deduct*). b) completely, (*declare, denude, deride*). *De-* is also added to verbs and their **derivatives** to form verbs and nouns means removal or
10 reversal (*decentralize; de-ice; demoralization*), (All the words in the table are verbs.

descend 降りる、由来する
deduct 差し引く、推論する
denude 裸にする、根こそぎにする
deride あざ笑う、ばかにする
demoralization 士気喪失

Table 4–2 de- Words

Word	Definition
demilitarize	to prohibit military forces or installations in an area
depend	to be affected, or decided, by other factors
depict	to represent in a picture or sculpture
deport	to expel from a country; especially, to remove into exile, to banish
depose	to remove someone from office or from a position of power
demilitarize	to prohibit military forces or installations in an area

in-

In- becomes *i-* before *gn*; *il-* before *l*; *im-* before *b* and *m*; and *ir-* before *r*. Don't confuse this *in-* with another *in-* that means "*in, within.*" These variations can mean "not," "with," "put into," "provide with," and "surround." To figure out the appropriate meaning, look at the context.

Table 4–3   *in-* Words *(also il-, im-, ir-,em-, en-)*

Word	Definition
ignorance	a lack of knowledge, learning, information, etc.
illiterate	someone who is unable to read and write
improbable	having a probability too low to inspire belief
inactive	not active
incessant	without interruption
inaudible	not be heard
illegal	not legal
immobile	not movable
immaterial	not important

un-

***Un-* is** added to adjectives and participles and their derivative nouns and adverbs, meaning a) *not*, pointing out the lack of a quality or state. b) the reverse of, with a suggestion of approval or disapproval or with some other special nuance.

participle　分詞

Table 4–4   *un-* Words

Word	Definition
unable	not able
undone	not done
unfair	not fair
unbuttoned	not buttoned

unreal	not real
unruly	not disciplined
unaware	not aware

pre-

Pre- means "before" in time, place, order, degree or importance. Examples of words with the *pre-* prefix include *preview* (view before) and *preamble* (introductory statement to a speech).

Table 4–5 Pre- Words

Word	Definition
prepay	to pay before
precut	to cut before
precool	to cool before
predate	to date before
prehistoric	prior to written history
predict	to say before something happens
pre-owned	used; owned before
preview	to see before/to view before
preset	to set before
prejudge	to judge before

More Common Prefixes

In addition to the most commonly used prefixes, English words use many other prefixes, also. Examples of these include *anti-* (against) and *con-* (with).

a-, anti-, dis, and more

Several prefixes mean "not" or "against": *a-, anti-, dis-,* and *in-* and its variations.

Table 4–6 Prefixes meaning "not" and "against"

Prefix	Meaning	Word	Definition
a	not, without	atypical	not typical
		amoral	without morals (neither moral nor immoral)
anti	opposite to, against	antibody	against body
		anti-Christian	opposed to Christianity
		anti-nuclear	opposed to nuclear power/weapons
dis	not	dislike	not like
		disagree	to not be in agreement
in (il, ir. im, ig)	not or without	inconsiderate	not sensitive to other's feelings
		illegible	not readable
		immodest	indecent (the opposite of modest)
		ignore	refuse to know or notice

co- con-, and sym-/syn-

Several prefixes mean "with" or "together."

Table 4–7 Prefixes Meaning "with" or "together"

Prefix	Meaning	Word	Definition
co	with, together	co-author	2 authors working together
		coalition	alliance for combined action
		co-worker	colleague, work together with
com, con col	with, together	combine	join together
		comfort	a state of physical well-being
		conjunction	act of joining together
		compact	neatly packed together
		collaborate	work together on a plan or project
sym, syn	together	synchronize	occur at the same time
		syndicate	a group of companies or people who combine
		synopsis	summary

Chapter 4

Location Prefixes

Just as some prefixes show number or degree (as will be explained later), other prefixes, such as *circum-*, indicate location or direction. If you know that *circum-* means "around," then you can figure out that the phrase *circumnavigate the globe* means "to go around the world." Table 4-8 shows more examples of this and other location/direction prefixes.

Table 4–8 Prefixes that Indicate Location or Direction			
Prefix	**Meaning**	**Word**	**Definition**
a, ad, ap	to, towards	approach	move toward
		address	speak to
cata	down	catacomb	underground room
		catalogue	an extensive list of items
circum	around	circumambulate	walk around
		circumference	outer boundary of a circle
		circumscribe	restrict
		circumvent	go around, avoid
hyper	over or above	hypercritical	excessively critical
		hyperactive	more active than normal
		hyperbaric	higher than normal atmospheric pressure
hypo	under or below	hypothermia	body temperature below normal
		hypodermic	beneath the skin
sub	under	subordinate	lower than or inferior to
		subterranean	underground

Numbers Prefixes

The Arabians gave us the symbols that represent numbers—1, 2, 3, 4, 5 and so on. The words used to speak or write these symbols—one, two, three, four, five, and so on—came from the Anglo-Saxons. The prefixes that indicate numbers came from the Greek and Latin.

Table 4–9 Number Prefixes

Prefix	Meaning	Word	Definition
uni (Latin)	1	unicycle	vehicle with one wheel
mono (Greek)		monologue	dramatic speech done by one actor
bi, *duo* (Latin)	2	bicycle	vehicle with two wheels
di (Greek)		duplex	house with two units
		dichotomy	division into two parts
tri (Latin or Greek)	3	tripod	three-legged stand
quad (Latin)	4	quadrangle	figure with four sides and four angles
tetra (Greek)		tetrahedron	a solid with four sides
penta (Greek)	5	pentagram	star-shaped figure with five points
hexa (Greek)	6	hexagon	figure with six sides
hepta (Greek)	7	heptagon	figure with seven sides and seven angles
oct (Greek or Latin)	8	octet	group of eight
nov (Latin)	9	novena	prayers said on nine straight days
deca (Latin or Greek)	10	decalogue	the Ten Commandments

Degree Prefixes

Some prefixes indicate the amount of something.

Table 4–10 Prefixes that Indicate Degree

Prefix	Meaning	Word	Definition
pan	all	pan-American	all of the Americas
		pandemic	widespread disease
poly	many	polyglot	knowing many languages
		polygon	figure with many sides
super	over, beyond, more than	supercilious	arrogant or overly proud

Chapter 4

ultra	beyond, excessive	ultramarine	deep blue
		ultraviolet	beyond the visible spectrum of light

Exercise

Answer these questions.

1. attractive, subtraction, traction and tractor. What does the prefix tract- mean? a. to go, to yield b. distance, from afar c. time d. to drag, draw Answer_____	2. audible, auditorium, audition and audience. What does the prefix audi- mean? a. between b. to believe c. to hear d. to go, to yield Answer_____
3. chronological, chronic, chronicle and anachronism. What does the prefix chrono- mean? a. circle b. to drag, draw c. time d. self Answer_____	4. benefit, benevolent, beneficiary and benediction. What does the prefix bene- mean? a. speak b. time c. good, well d. against, opposite Answer_____
5. intermission, intermittent, international and intercept. What does the prefix inter- mean? a. sound b. outside c. between d. against, opposite Answer_____	6. If the prefix dict- means "speak," a book that lists and explains the meanings of a language is called a _____. a. dictionary b. predict c. diction d. verdict Answer_____

Chapter 4

7. If the prefix multi- means many, if there are a great many people gathered together, it is known as a _____. a. multiply b. subtraction c. vital d. multitude	8. If the prefix chrono- means time, a record of events in the order in which they occur is called a _____. a. chronicle b. chronological c. audition d. intercept
Answer_____	Answer_____
9. If the prefix vita- means life, when one is full of life one if full of _____. a. vitamins b. audience c. traction d. vitality	10. If the prefix audi- means to hear, if you hear something clearly it is _____. a. auditorium b. audience c. audition d. audible
Answer_____	Answer_____

Chapter 5
The Greeks and Latins

英語はゲルマン語派であるアングロサクソン語をベースとして、多くの言語の影響を受けています。11世紀にノルマン人がイングランドを征服し、大量にフランス語が流入しました。16～17世紀には文人たちがギリシャ語やラテン語の文献から学術用語を中心に多数の単語を借用しました。本章では、よく使われるギリシャ語とラテン語起源の接頭辞を見ていきましょう。接頭辞の起源がギリシャ語であるかラテン語であるかということは覚える必要はありませんが、通常、ギリシャ語の接頭辞はギリシャ語の語根と、ラテン語の接頭辞はラテン語の語根と結びつくということは覚えておいてください。

Greek Prefixes

The Greek language gave English many of the most common prefixes. These prefixes open up a whole new world of words that you may find yourself using a great deal in your life. By learning the meaning of **roots** and **prefixes**, you will be able to figure out many commonly used words. Think about these examples!

a. *Astronaut* means "star sailor." It uses the Greek prefix *astro*, which means "star" and the Greek root *nautes, which* means "sailor." Its English definition is "space traveler."

b. *Autonomy* means "self-rule." It contains the Greek prefix *auto,* which means "self" and the Greek root *nomos*, which means "law." Its English definition is "self government" or "independence."

c. *Synchronize* means "timed together." It uses the prefix *syn-* (together) and the root *chronos* (time). If you *synchronize* watches, you make them agree in time. Some of these prefixes can also functions as roots, depending on their placement in the word. More on roots later on.

Table 5–1 Greek Prefixes		
Prefix	**Meaning**	**Example Words**
arch	chief	archbishop
arche, *archae*	ancient, original	archetype
		archaeology
auto	self	automobile
bio	life	biography
chromo, *chroma*	color	chromosphere
chron	time	chronological
eu	good	eulogize
		euphonious
		euphoria

The adjective *cosmopolitan* gets its meaning from *cosmo*, which means "world," and *polit*, which means "state or region," thus it means "common to all or many parts of the world" or "not local or national."

Table 5–1 Greek Prefixes (continued)		
Prefix	**Meaning**	**Example Words**
micro	small	microbe
		microfilm
mis	wrong	misdemeanor
		misspell
		mistake
peri	around	perimeter
phil	love	philanthropy

phob	fear	claustrophobia
pseudo	false	pseudoscience
tele	distance	telephone
		telecommunication
		telepathy
theo	God	theology

Latin Prefixes

Besides the Greek language, Latin has also given English some extremely useful prefixes. Many of the number prefixes, as well as *a-* (to or toward) for example, are Latin prefixes. Whether any particular group of letters is a prefix or not depends on whether that group appears at the front of the word. Some of these prefixes can also be used as *roots*. More on roots later on! Table 5-2 lists a few of them.

Table 5–2 Latin Prefixes

Prefix	Meaning	Example Words
ag, agen, act, agi, agit	motion, to shake, to drive, to do, to act, to lead, to conduct, to guide	action, activate, activity, navigate
ante, ant	before, in front of, prior to, forward	advance, antecede, anteroom, anticipant
bene, ben, beni	good, well	benediction, benefactor beneficial
contra, contro, counter, contre	against, opposed to, opposite, contrary	encounter, contraband, contradict, counteract, counterculture
cur	to run	current
e	out	elongate
ex	out	exchange

infra	under	infrared
inter	between	intercom
mal, *male*	bad, evil	malodorous
		malevolent
ob	toward	obedient
ob	in the way	obstruction
per	through	perambulate
post	after	postpone

Anglo-Saxon Prefixes

The 100 most often used words in the English language all come from Anglo-Saxon. And, of course, the Anglo-Saxons got many of their words from the Romans; so where these prefixes originated is hard to determine.

√ In or into:
  illuminate (bring in light)
  import (bring in from another country)
  irradiate (let x-rays into)

√ Not:
  illiterate (not able to read)
  immodest (not modest)
  irregular (not regular)

You generally will not have a problem figuring out which meaning these prefixes draw on for any single word, unless you confuse the adjectives *irrefutable*, which means "cannot be disproved," and *irresolute*, which means "indecisive."

Don't fall into the trap of thinking that because every-

disprove 〜に反証する
indecisive 決断力のない、優柔不断な
trap わな

body uses it, it must be right. This example shows how wrong "everybody" can be.

Correct: *Regardless* of the thunderstorm, I'm going swimming.
Incorrect: *Irregardless* of the thunderstorm, I'm going swimming.

Irregardless is not a real word—attaching the ir- prefix doesn't change that. *Regardless* means "without regard" or "unmindful," which is what people who use *irregardless* really want to say.

unmindful	不注意な、無頓着な

Double Duty Words

Some words, in their own right, work as prefixes, modifying or changing a specific word. Consider the following:

in one's own right	自分自身の能力で、独立して

- √ *Counter* means "opposed to" or "contrary." When used as a prefix, it keeps this meaning and, as a result, essentially negates the meaning of the word it's attached to. Examples of *counter* used as a prefix include *counterintuitive,* (not intuitive) and *counterproductive* (not productive).

intuitive	直観的な

- √ *Under* means "beneath" or "below." Examples of *under* used as a prefix include *underage,* (not old enough), *underscore* (emphasize, by drawing a line under), and *underhanded* (sneaky).

sneaky	こそこそする、卑劣な

- √ *Over* means "higher than," "superior" or "excessive." Examples of *over* used as a prefix include

Chapter 5

overarching (dominant), *overreaching* (reaching above or beyond), and *overdrawn* (over your bank balance).

You shouldn't have too much trouble understanding what these dual-purpose words/prefixes mean.

dual-purpose　２つの目的を兼ねた

Exercise

Answer these questions.	
1. If the prefix dec- means ten, the Tenth Month is also called _____ (the Roman year began with March). a. December　　b. May c. February　　d. July Answer_____	2. If the prefix sept- means seven, a person seventy years old or between seventy to seventy-nine is called _____. a. quintet　　b. septuagenarian c. Pentecost　　d. quadriliteral Answer_____
3. If the prefix pent- means five, a government ruled by five people is called _____. a. tricycle　　b. hexapod c. pentarchy　　d. quadruplets Answer_____	4. If the prefix chrono- means time, an illness lasting for a very long time is said to be _____. a. chronological　　b. chronicle c. anachronism　　d. chronic Answer_____
5. If the prefix bi- means two, cutting something into two pieces is called _____. a. bicycle　　b. pentagram c. sextus　　d. bisecting Answer_____	6. If the prefix oct- means eight, the Eighth Month is also called _____ (the Roman year began with March). a. October　　b. September c. December　　d. February Answer_____

7. If the prefix demo- means people, a government that is ruled by representatives elected by an entire group of people in a population is called a _____. a. democracy b. demography c. epidemic d. demagogue	8. If the prefix cyclo- means circle, something that occurs in cycles (or circles) is _____. a. bicycle b. cyclical c. encyclopedia d. cycle
Answer_____	Answer_____
9. f the prefix demo- means people, the study of peoples' statistics regarding birth, death and disease is known as _____. a. democracy b. epidemic c. demagogue d. demography	10. If the prefix bene- means good or well, when you do a favor or something good for someone else, then the person you give it to is known as the _____. a. benefit b. benevolent c. benediction d. beneficiary
Answer_____	Answer_____

Chapter 6
Roots

第4〜5章では「語彙力アップの秘密」その1としてさまざまな接頭辞を見てきました。本章と次章で扱うのは語根です。これが「語彙力アップの秘密」その2です。語根とは単語の意味の核となる、それ以上分解不可能な部分のことです。語根という「根っこ」に接頭辞や接尾辞などの枝葉がついて1つの単語ができあがっているのです。語根の意味を知っていれば、未知の単語の正確な訳はわからなくても、だいたいの意味を把握することが可能です。また、単語を覚えるときも、同じ語根を持つ単語をまとめて覚えることで単語数を飛躍的に増やすことができます。

Here Is Secret #2

A **word root** is the most basic form of a word that is able to carry an exact description, thought or meaning.

5　In *linguistics* (the study of languages), English language roots are officially known as **morphemes** and defined as the basic unit of a word. They carry a significant part of origin substance and cannot be shortened into any smaller parts.

10　Sometimes the term "root" is used to describe the word minus its word change endings, but with its original endings in place. **Inflection** (word change) is a changed form of a word to point to grammar (language rules), such as **gender** (male or female), **tense**
15　(past, present or future), **number** or **person**.

morpheme　形態素

substance　実体、内容

The root of a word is a unit of meaning and, as such, it is an idea, though it can usually be represented in writing, as a word would be. As an example, the root of the verb "running" is "run," and the root of the adjective "amplified" is "ampli-," since those words are clearly *derived* (taken) from the root forms by simple suffixes that do not clearly change the roots. The English language has very little *inflection* and so a fondness to have words that are very close to their own roots.

However, more difficult inflection, as well as other linguistic processes, can make the root *obscure* (difficult to understand). For example, the root of "mice" is "mouse" (a suitable but different word), and the root of "interrupt" is "rupt," which is not an actual word in English and only appears in changed forms (e.g. rupture, corrupt). Knowing about these cases will aid the hungry vocabulary builder.

The Basics of Roots

You need to know a few things about how roots work, in order to use roots to figure out a word's meaning. A root is the basic element of a word, and it is the base on which the meaning of a word is built. Many roots are real words on their own right: for example, *graph* (a diagram) and *term* (fixed time or date).

Although these roots can have other elements, they don't need other elements to be complete. However, most roots do need other elements. For example, the root *archy* (government) and *dox* (opinion or belief) need to be combined with other word elements, like

---

as such それ (unit of meaning) 自体で

fondness 好み

prefixes, suffixes or even other roots:

dyarchy: a government by two rulers, from the prefix *di-* (meaning two) and the root *archy* (meaning government).

anarchist: someone who rejects the need for a system of government in society and proposes its abolition. From the prefix *an-* (meaning without or no), the root *archy* (meaning government) and the suffix *-ist* (meaning one who.)

orthodox: Correct or sound in doctrine; holding the commonly accepted faith, and established doctrines, from the prefix *ortho-* (meaning right or true) and the root *dox* (meaning opinion or belief)

- **Some roots form whole words by themselves.** For instance, *vent* means "opening to allow air to enter"; and *audio* means "sound" or "hearing." Although these roots make words in and of themselves, you can also combine them with other word elements (prefixes and suffixes) to make new words, as in the following:

Root + Word Element	New Word	Definition
vent + ilate	ventilate	open to air
audio + ible	audible	able to be heard

- **Some roots must be combined with other elements to make new words.** Consider:

ruler 支配者

in and of oneself それ自体として

Root + Word Element	New Word	Definition
capit + al	capital	most important
carn + age	carnage	slaughter
chrono + logy	chronology	timeline

When you can put together the meaning of a root with the meaning of a prefix and a suffix, you can easily understand the meaning of words.

Joining Roots to Roots

You might wonder whether a word element is acting as a prefix or as a root when you come across words made by joining two roots. The truth is that, although some word elements are always prefixes and others are suffixes always found at the end of a word, at times you can find roots in any position, and it doesn't matter whether the root is at the beginning, in the middle, or at the end of a word, as long as you understand the word's meaning. Here are some examples:

- *chron* (time) + *meter* (measure) make up *chronometer*, an instrument for measuring time.
- *cal* (beauty) + *graph* (to write) make up *calligraphy*, which means "graceful penmanship."

graceful 優雅な、上品な
penmanship ペン習字、書法

Roots for Measuring

The Greeks gave English many roots for measuring things like distances and depth. Several of these roots mean the same thing. For instance, *macro* and *mega* both mean "large."

Table 6–1 Greek Roots for Measurements

Root	Meaning	Example Word
arc, arc, arci, arch, arch	bow, a curved structure	arcade, archer, archway
arch, archi, arch	chief, principal leader, first	archduke, architect, archrival
chromo, chroma	color	chromatic
chron, chrono	time	chronicle, anachronic
gero, geri, ger, geronto, geront	old age, old man, old people	geriatrician, geriatric
horo, hour	hour, time; period of time, season, any limited time	encore, horoscope hourly
meter	measure	altimeter, metric
ne, neo	new, recent, current, young	neoclassic, neology neophyte

Common Roots

A root, as its name suggests, is a word or word part from which other words grow, usually through the addition of prefixes and suffixes. The root of the word *vocabulary*, for example, is *voc*, a Latin root meaning "word" or "name." This root also appears in the words *advocacy*, *convocation*, *evocative*, *vocal*, and *vociferous*.

advocacy 擁護、弁護
convocation 会議（の招集）
evocative [adj] 記憶を呼び起こす、感情に訴える
vociferous 大声で叫ぶ、騒々しい

The table below identifies and shows 30 of the most common Greek and Latin roots.

Table 6–2 Greek and Latin Roots

Root	Meaning	Example Words
aster (G)	star	asteroid, astronomy, asterisk
audi (L)	hear	audible, audience, audio
auto (G)	self	automatic, autopsy, autism, autistic
bene (L)	good, well	benefit, benign, benevolent

Chapter 6

bio (G)	life	biography, biology, antibiotic
chrono (G)	time	chronic, chronological, synchronize
dict (L)	say, talk, speak	dictate, diction, predict, contradict
duc (L)	lead, bringing	deduce, deduct, produce, producer
gen (L)	give birth	gene, generate, genetic, congenial
geo (G)	earth, land, soil	geography, geology
graph (G)	write, to describe	autograph, graph, graffiti, graphic
jur (L)	right, law, legal	jury, justice, adjure, conjure
log (G)	talk, speak, word	logic, logical, logo
luc (L)	light, shine	elucid, elucidate, illuminate
manu, man, mani (L)	hand	manual, manure, command, maintain
mand, mend (L)	defect, blemish	amends, amendment, recommend
mis, mit (L)	send, to let go	admissible, missile, transmission
omni (L)	all, every	omniscient, omnipresent, omnivorous
path (G)	feel, sensation	empathy, pathetic, hemopathy
phil (G)	love	philosophy, bibliophile
photo (G)	light	photograph, photon
port (L)	carry	export, portable
qui (t) (L)	quiet, rest	acquit, tranquil
scrib, script (L)	write	ascribe, script
sens, sent (L)	feel	resent, sensitive
tele (G)	far off	telecast, telephone
terr (L)	earth	terrain, territory
vac (L)	empty	evacuate, vacate
vid, vis (L)	see	visible, video

Exercise

These problems ask definitions on Greek & Latin Roots.

1. Directions: Find the matching squares.

therm	join	space or stars	cogn
spit	paper	breathe, life, spirit	cent
astro	foot	100	chart
ped	born with, knowing	hot or heat	junct

Answer here:

1. _____ = _____   2. _____ = _____
3. _____ = _____   4. _____ = _____
5. _____ = _____   6. _____ = _____
7. _____ = _____   8. _____ = _____

2. FOCUS: pos

Prefix	Root	Suffix
com- (with, together)		
de- (away, down)		
ex- (out, away, from)	pos/posit (place, put)	-ion (state, quality, act)
im- (in, into, not)		
op- (against)		

Directions:

In column A, identify the parts of speech by circling roots and then underlining prefixes and suffixes.

Match each word to its correct meaning in column B.

Column A
1. expose
2. composition
3. deposit
4. imposition
5. opposition

42

Column B

____ a. an unjust burden placed on someone.

____ b. to put down or in a safe place.

____ c. an arrangement or putting together of parts.

____ d. the act of resistance or action against.

____ e. to place something where it can be seen.

Chapter 7
The Source of Origin

前章に引き続き、本章でもさまざまな語根を学びます。本章では自然界に関連する語根、信念・概念に関連する語根、製造・移動に関連する語根など、カテゴリー別に紹介していきます。これまでなんとなく覚えていた単語も、語根の意味を視覚的にイメージすることによって単語全体の意味がより鮮明に理解できるようになることでしょう。ここにあげたそれぞれの語根の単語例のほかにもっと知りたいという方は、語根や接頭辞・接尾辞で引けるようになっている語源辞典をぜひ活用してください。意外な単語が同じ語根を持っていることがわかったりすることもあって、パラパラと眺めているだけでも楽しいものです。

The Natural World

Below are some Greek roots and words formed from them that explain the natural world.

Table 7–1　Roots that explain the Natural World

Root	Meaning	Example Words
bio, bi, bia,	life, living, live, alive	biography, autobiography
gen	birth	generate
gyn	woman	gynecologist
helio, heli	sun	heliotrope, heliocentric
ichty	fish	ichthism, ichthismus
phyt	plant; growth	acrophyte
polis, polit, poli	method of government; citizenship, government	cosmopolitan, apolitical, politician
pyr	fire, burn; heat	pyromaniac
ornith	bird	ornithology
soma	body, mass	somatic, psychosomatic
therm	heat	thermometer

zoo	animal, life	zoology, megazooid

Belief and Thoughts

These roots are useful in the most unexpected situations.

Table 7–2 Greek Roots for Belief and Thoughts

Root	Meaning	Example Words
arch	chief, leader, ruler	archangel, monarch, archaic, archenemy
crac, *crat*	rule, ruler	autocrat, democracy, bureaucrat
gam	marriage	polygamy, bigamy, monogamy
graph	writing	biography, telegraph, geography
iso	equal, identical	isolate
logy, *ology*	branch of knowledge	entomology
nom	rule	autonomy
onym, *nym*	name, word	pseudonym, synonym, acronym
orama	view	panorama
path	feeling, suffering	sympathy, apathy, empathy, telepathy
psych	soul, spirit, mind	psychology, psychic, psychobiography
theo	god, deity	theology, atheist, polytheism

Latin Roots

As the ancient Romans conquered most of Europe, their language spread throughout the region. Over time, the Latin spoken in different areas grew into separate languages, including Italian, French, Spanish, and Portuguese. These languages are considered "sisters," as they all came down from Latin, their "mother" language.

Many Latin words came into English directly, though, too. Priests from Rome brought religious vocabulary as well as Christianity to England at the start of the

priest 司祭、神父

Chapter 7

6th century. From the Middle Ages onward, many scientific, scholarly, and legal terms were borrowed from Latin.

During the 17th and 18th centuries, dictionary writers
5 and grammarians generally felt that English was an imperfect language whereas Latin was perfect. In order to improve the language, they deliberately made up a lot of English words from Latin words. For example, *fraternity*, from Latin *fraternitas*, was
10 thought to be better than the native English word *brotherhood*.

Many English words can be traced back to Latin. The following table lists some common Latin roots.

	Table 7–3 Latin Roots	
Root	**Meaning**	**Example Words**
act, ag	do, act, drive	active
am, ami	love, like	amorous
alt	high	altitude
anim	life, mind, spirit, anger	animus, animal
annu, enni	yearly	annual
auc, aug, aut	to originate, to increase	augment
aud, audit, aur	to hear	audible
arbitr, arbiter	to judge,	arbitrator
art	craft, skill	artist
brev	short	brevity, abbreviate, brief
cad, cap, cas, ceiv	to take, to hold	receive
cert	sure, to trust	certificate
cede, ceed, cess	to go, yield	exceed
clam, claim	to call out,	clamor
cent	one hundred	century

cert	sure, to trust	certificate
corp	body	corporate
cre, cresc, cret	to grow	create
cred	to believe	incredible
corp	body	corporate
cog, gnos	to know	recognize
cour, cur, curr, curs	to run, course	occur
cont	to join, unite	continue

Making and Moving Roots

The Roman Empire, during its peak, included all of Eastern and Western Europe (including the British Islands) and went into Northern Africa and Western Asia. The Roman Empire was known for its strong, centralized government and building of roads, irrigation systems and canals. So it's no wonder that many English words related to making and moving stuff use Latin roots. The root *fact*, which means "to make" gives the English language words like *factory* (a place where goods are produced) and *manufacture* (to make for use). Below are other Latin roots that relate to doing something.

irrigation 灌溉
canal 運河

Table 7-4 Latin Roots for Making and Moving

Root	Meaning	Example Words
duc, duct	lead	induce, deduce, seduction, conduct
fer	carry	transfer
funct	perform	functional
grad, gress	step	gradual, progression, transgression
ject	throw	inject, reject, subject, projection
pel, puls	push, move	pedal, pedometer, centipede, gastropod
scrib	write	scribble, inscribe

Chapter 7

Other Latin Roots

You can find several other Latin roots in the English language. Consider the following examples:

- *Annual* (yearly) uses the Latin root *ann/enn*, which means "year." *Anniversary* (the yearly celebration of a particular date) uses the same root, as does *biennial* (occurring every two years) and *biannual* (occurring twice in the same year).

- The word *annihilate* uses the Latin root *nihil*, which means "nothing." To *annihilate* something is to do away with it entirely. The word *nihilism*, a belief that life has no meaning or value, also comes from this root.

  do away with X　Xを処分する、排除する

- The word *pendulous* which means "drooping" uses the Latin root *pend*, which means "weigh." The word *pendulum* (an object that swings back and forth freely from a fixed point) also uses this root. The following table lists other Latin roots, including those that describe size, amount, and location. As you read, consider how you would use some of these words in your daily life.

  drooping　垂れ下がっている
  weigh　重さがある、重荷になる

Table 7–5 Other Latin Roots		
Root	**Meaning**	**Example Words**
alto, alt, alti	high, highest, tall, lofty	altar, alter, altitude
centro, centr, centri,	center	acentric, central, eccentric
dog, dox	opinion, doctrine, decree; praise	dogma, orthodox
fin	end, last, limit	affinity, infinity, definite
magn	large	magnify, magnificent, magnate

Chapter 7

med	middle	median, medicine, medical
multi	much, many	multiply, multitude
omni	all, every	omniscient, omnidirectional
sed, sedat, sid, sess	sit, sitting	sedate, sedentary, session
ten, tent, tin, tain, tainment, tenance, tinence	hold, grasp, have	abstain, appertain, container, continue, discontent, obtain, retain, tenant, tennis
term	end, last, final boundary	terminal, exterminate
vid, vis	to see	visual, view

Exercise

Match the root to its definition.

Root	Definition	Answer here
1. act	animal life, a living being	
2. acu, acr, ac	year, yearly	
3. alt	water	
4. anima, anim	weapon; implement of war	
5. ann, enn	consider, judge; spectator	
6. aqua	skill, handicraft, trade	
7. arm	hearing, listening, perception of sounds	
8. arbitr, arbiter	high, highest, tall, lofty	
9. art	sharp, to sharpen, point; needle, pin	
10. aud	to set in motion	

Chapter 8
Suffixes

「語彙力アップの秘密」その1が接頭辞、その2が語根と来れば、その3が接尾辞であるということはもうおわかりでしょう。接尾辞には「語の品詞を決める」という重要な働きがあります。品詞は英文の構造を理解するためのヒントの1つですから、どの接尾辞がつくとどの品詞になるのかという知識はリーディングにおいても非常に役立ちます。中学校で習ったときは接尾辞だという意識はなかったかもしれませんが、名詞の複数形につける -s や動詞の3人称単数現在形につける -s、過去形・過去分詞形につける -d/-ed も接尾辞です。それぞれの接尾辞があらわす品詞を覚えたら、品詞の機能についても文法書で復習しておきましょう。

Here Is Secret #3

Prefixes and suffixes are called affixes—they are attached to a word root to produce a new word. However, suffixes go one step further than prefixes in that a suffix can affect how a word works in a sentence by determining the word's part of speech. By adding a suffix, you can make a verb from a noun, or an adjective or an adverb from a verb. Suffixes can also show amount or quantity.

Some suffixes are used so frequently that you may not even think of them—much less recognize them—as suffixes. These include *-d/-ed*, which are used to indicate tense on a verb, and *-s/es*, which are used to show number.

Chapter 8

People's Favorites

Which suffixes are most important? Some people sponsor *-ness, -ity,* and *-ful* and certainly *-ate, -less* and *-ly* have their fans. I like *-ment, -ence/-ance,* *-able/-ible* and *-ion*. The following table shows what these suffixes mean and gives examples of their use.

Table 8-1 Suffixes: *-ment, -ence/-ance, -able/-ible* and *-ion*

Suffix	Meaning	Example Words
-ment	result of, means of, act of; place of action	abolishment, accomplishment achievement
-ence, -ance, -ency	state, quality, or condition of	confidence, fluency, influence, insolence
-able	capacity, fitness to do, suitable	accountable, adorable, amicable
-ible	can be done, worthy of being,	audible, edible, flexible
-ion, -sion, tion	act	infection, rebellion, collection

The difference between the suffix *-able/-ible* and the other suffixes in the table is that *-able/-ible* creates adjectives. The other suffixes create nouns. Another suffix that creates nouns is *-age*, which means "place of" (*orphan*age = a place of orphans), "an act of" (*breakage* = the act of breaking) and "charge for" (*postage* = charge for post).

orphan 孤児

Showing Action

The suffixes *-ate, -en, -ite,* and *-ize* all mean "to make" or "to do." Words using these suffixes include *alienate, liberate, weaken, moisten, unite, ignite, visualize* and *sanitize*.

Suffixes have multiple meanings and can change the definition of a word. For example, the suffix *-ite*, when it means "to make" or "to do," creates verbs.

However, *-ite* can also mean "one who." In this case, the suffix creates a noun (*socialite*, for example).

Changing Tense: -d/-ed and -ing

Suffixes can change a word's tense (or time). Adding the suffix *-d* or *-ed* to the end of a verb changes it from present tense to past tense. Adding the suffix *-ing* changes a present tense verb into a present participle or gerund.

present participle 現在分詞
gerund 動名詞

Table 8–2 Suffixes and Verb Tense

Word	Past Tense	Present Participle/Gerund
live	lived	living
fasten	fastened	fastening
run	ran	running
walk	walked	walking

Note that the past tense of "run" is not formed with *-d* or *-ed*. Many verbs, such as *am/was, buy/bought*, and *sell/sold*, form irregular past tenses. The suffix *-ing,* however, works for all verbs.

Tense is a form of a verb that shows time, action, or state of being. Verbs are the only words in English that can show tense. English verbs have six tenses: *present* (walk), *past* (walked), *future* (will walk), *present perfect* (have walked), *past perfect* (had walked), *future perfect* (will have walked). For four of the six tenses you also add a "helping verb" such as *have* or *will*.

helping verb 助動詞

Adding Amounts: -s, -es and others

To show numbers you use suffixes. In specific, you

use the following suffixes: *-s* and *-es*. By putting these suffixes to a singular noun (such as *house, tree, boat,* and *box,* for instance), you make the noun plural (*houses, trees, boats* and *boxes*). However, adding a simple *-s* or *-es* does not make all English plurals. Sometimes the ending of the word is changed in other ways. Take the word *child*, for example. When plural, it becomes *children*. The word *ox* becomes *oxen*.

Don't forget the suffixes that produce adjectives show amount in a more slight way. *-ful, -ose/ous,* and *-y* all mean "full of."

- *-y* makes *risky* (full of danger) and *wily* (full of sly tricks).
- *-ful* gives you *healthful* (full of physical well-being) and *cheerful* (full of gladness).
- *-ose/ous* leads to *morose* (full of sadness) and *perilous* (full of danger).

sly　ずるい、狡猾な
trick　たくらみ、策略
well-being　幸福、福祉、厚生

Almost every English word can take at least one (or more) suffixes. There are descriptive suffixes (they show states of being), suffixes for comparison, and suffixes that point to people and what they do.

Suffixes that Show a State of Being: -cy, -dom, -ant, -ness, and more

How do we describe what we see, feel, taste, or meet? Being aware of yourself and of your surroundings is your *state of being*. These suffixes include *-ant/-ent, -cy, -dom, -hood, -mony, -ness, -sis, -tic, -ship,* and *-ty*. See the table below:

Table 8–3 Suffixes that Indicate State of Being

Suffix	Meaning	Example Words
-acy, -cy	state, quality, condition, or act of	adequacy, democracy
-dom, -domo, -domat	house, home	domain, domestic, dominance
-ant	a person who, a thing which	abundant, accelerant
-ent	signifying action or being	abhorrent, achievement
-mony	action, result of an action or condition	patrimony, sanctimony
-osis, -sis, -sia, -sy	actor, process, condition, or state of; result of	hypnosis, metamorphosis
-ic	pertaining to; of the nature of, like	electronic, epidemic, logic, rhetoric, historic
-ship	state or condition	friendship, governorship

Relating to or Showing Likeness: -ac, -al, -esque, -ish, and others

The word *majesty,* in relation to a king, means "imposing and impressive." Many common suffixes indicate similarities: *-esque, -ish, -oid,* and *-wise,* for example. Other common suffixes, like *-ac, -al,* and *-ile*, mean "relating to." Overall these suffixes enable you to describe your thoughts, feelings and the things you see and experience. See the table below:

imposing　堂々とした、人目を引く

Table 8–4 Suffixes Showing Likeness or Comparisons

Suffix	Meaning	Example Words
-ac	related to, pertaining to	amnesiac, cardiac, insomniac, maniac
-al, -ial, -eal	pertaining to, like, relating to, of	abnormal, aboriginal, acquittal, alphabetical

-oid, -oidal, -odic	like, resembling, similar to, form	android, asteroid, humanoid
-age	quality of, process, function, condition	acreage, appendage, courage, dosage
-ile, -il	ability to, capable of, suitable for; like	agile, docile, facile, fragile, juvenile
-ine	similar to, resembling, characterized by	alpine, aquiline, bovine, canine
-ly-, -lys, -lysis, -lytic	to loosen; dissolving, dissolution	analysis, analyze, catalyst
-ory	of or relating to, resembling	accessory, derogatory

Exercise

Match the suffixes to their definitions and words.
Write your answers in the boxes.

Suffixes	Definitions	Words
1. -cy		
2. -dom		
3. -ment		
4. -ent		
5. -ence		
6. -ac		
7. -oid		
8. -age		
9. -able		
10. -al		

Chapter 8

Definitions

a. result of, means of
b. resembling, similar to
c. pertaining to, of the kind of
d. arts, sciences
e. function, condition
f. state, quality
g. fitness to do
h. action or being
i. condition, act of
j. master, lord

Words

(i) educational
(ii) attainment
(iii) asteroid
(iv) fluency
(v) desirable
(vi) discourage
(vii) legacy
(viii) domestic
(ix) maniac
(x) treatment

Chapter 9
More Suffixes

前章に続いて、さらにいろいろな接尾辞を学んでいきましょう。動詞に -er をつけると「〜する人」という意味になるのはご存知だと思いますが、「人」をあらわす接尾辞はほかにもあります。「人」をあらわす接尾辞が「場所」や「状態」をあらわすこともあります。また、接尾辞は品詞を決める働きがあるということは前章でも説明しましたが、本章では名詞をつくる接尾辞を中心に具体例を見ていきます。

People

A lot of suffixes relate to people: who they are, what they do, where they live, and what they are like. The suffix *-er*, for example, is useful because it means "one who does or deals with." This suffix, when added to many verbs, can show occupation. A *worker* is someone who works; a *teacher* is someone who teaches. A *baker* is someone who makes cake; a *buyer* is someone who buys items. The suffixes *-or, -ar, -ary, -ian, -ier,* and *-ist* also do the same job as *-er*. The following table lists the suffixes that point out a person who is something, does something, or deals with something. Because they all refer to people, all the words in the table are nouns.

Table 9–1   Suffixes related to People and their Positions

Suffix	Meaning	Example Words
-ar	pertaining to, of the nature of	circular, popular, scholar, exemplar, insular
-ary	a person who, a place where, a thing which	adversary, anniversary, dictionary

-arian	a person who, a thing that	agrarian, aquarian, authoritarian, barbarian
-ian	belonging to, coming from	academician, avian, custodian, historian

The suffix *-ar* is primarily used in words that end in *-le*. To use this suffix, you usually change the *-le* to *-ul* and then add *-ar*. Think about the following examples:

angle → angular
circle → circular
muscle → muscular

Often, words that end with *-ist* describe people who engage in particular hobbies or careers. The *-ite* suffix generally indicates something geographical about a person. A Muscovite, for example, is a person who lives in Moscow. The following table lists a few examples of nouns that use these suffixes.

Table 9–2 Examples of *ist* and *ite*

Word	Definition
artist	one who practices any of the arts
biologist	one who studies life
soloist	someone who performs solo
capitalist	one using or possessing capital
meteorologist	one who studies the weather
numismatist	one who deals with or collects coins
philatelist	one who deals with or collects stamps
psychologist	counselor
socialite	person who socializes on a grand scale

Place or Condition

These suffixes are good to know because they appear in many words and expressions you use every day.

Table 9–3 Suffixes related to Place or Condition		
Suffix	**Meaning**	**Example Words**
-arium -aria	a place for	aquarium, planetarium
-esce, -escent	beginning to be	adolescent, convalescent
-ese	of, belonging to, from a place	academese, legalese
-fy	make, do, build	dehumidify, falsify
-id	meaning, state	avid, florid
-ism, -ismus	belief in, practice of	alcoholism, communism
-itis	inflammation, burning, sensation	appendicitis, tonsillitis
-ive	tending to; of the quality of	cursive, festive
-tude	state, quality, condition of	altitude, gratitude
-ure	an act or result, result of the act of	composure, literature

Knowing suffixes lets you do more than figure out the meaning of unfamiliar words. With an understanding of suffixes—what they mean and how they affect the root word—you can find out the following:

- **A word's part of speech:** Knowing the part of speech you are dealing with helps you figure out how to use the word in a sentence.
- **The number:** Some suffixes are a sign of number or degree—how many or how much. More than one? More or less? Suffixes can tell you the answers to these questions.

Parts of Speech

English has eight parts of speech. They are:
- *Nouns:* Words that name a person, place, thing, or idea (*Tokyo, sumo, democracy*). Nouns like *David, Naoko* and *Japan*—names of people and places—are capitalized and called *proper nouns*.

- ***Pronouns:*** Words that take the place of a noun or another pronoun (*I, me, you, she, who, they*). **Possessive pronouns** like *my, mine, its, yours, theirs*, and *ours* show ownership.

- ***Verbs:*** Words that name an action or describe a state of being (*run, seem*).

- ***Adverbs:*** Words that describe verbs, adjectives, or other adverbs (*yesterday, below, happily, partly*).

- ***Adjectives:*** Words that describe nouns and pronouns (*red, more, second, several*).

- ***Conjunctions:*** Words that connect words or groups of words and show how they are related (*and, or, for, but, after, although, because*).

- ***Prepositions:*** Words that link a noun or pronoun to another word in the sentence (*by, about, behind, above, across, at*).

- ***Interjections:*** Words that show strong emotions (*Oh! Wow!*).

A Word's Function

To figure out how to use a new word, you need to know how a word should work in a sentence. And to know that, you need to figure out the word's **part of speech**. Is it a noun or a verb? Or is it an adjective or adverb? So how do you know what part of speech a word is? Well, you can look up the word in a dictionary to find out the part of speech, but that is a lot of

Chapter 9

trouble. Luckily, specific suffixes almost always make the new word the same part of speech: adding a *-y,* for example, makes just about any word an adjective.

The following sections list most of the more common suffixes according to what part of speech they make a word when added to it. If you can remember these basic suffixes and speech parts, you should have little trouble figuring out how to use words formed with these suffixes.

Not every word that ends with a specific suffix is the same part of speech. The suffix *-ly,* for example, is often used to make adverbs (*dutifully, happily, normally* and so on), but you can find *-ly* at the end of other words that aren't adverbs, such as *rely* (verb), *firefly* (noun), and *ghastly* (adjective).

rely 頼る、当てにする
firefly 蛍
ghastly 恐ろしい、ぞっとするような

Suffixes and Nouns

Nouns are persons (*Naoko, mom, girl*), place (*Tokyo, house, park*), things (*car, tree, pencil*), and concepts or ideas (*beauty, honesty, truth*). The suffixes that turn words into nouns include the following:

-ance
-ful
-ity
-men
-ness
-sion/tion
-age

Chapter 9

Whenever you see these suffixes at the end of a word, chances are you're looking at a noun. Here are some example sentences that use the nouns created by suffixes:

5
- The lack of any other options made her *acceptance* (agreement or approval) of the original plan certain.
- When she told her date that the evening was only slightly more interesting than he was, she said a
10 *mouthful* (comment rich in meaning).
- The *unity* (state of acting or being as one) of the members was never in doubt, even though each represented a different region.

Exercise

Match the suffixes to their definitions and words.

Suffix	Meaning	Words
1. -ary		
2. -ist		
3. -ar		
4. -id		
5. -arian		
6. -ly		
7. -esce		
8. -fy		
9. -arium		
10. -ism		

Chapter 9

Meaning

a. one who believes in, one who is engaged in
b. pertaining to, tending to
c. make, do, build, cause
d. loosening, dissolving
e. belief in, practice of
f. a person who, a thing that
g. a place for, abounding in
h. beginning to be, becoming
i. pertaining to, of the nature of
j. a person who, a place where, a thing which

Words

(i) hypnotism   (ii) popular   (iii) barbarian
(iv) adversary   (v) florescent   (vi) planetarium
(vii) paralysis   (viii) diversify   (ix) florid
(x) terrorist

Chapter 10
Suffixes, Parts of Speech, and Spelling

接尾辞に品詞を決める働きがあることはすでに学びました。前章までは主に名詞をつくる接尾辞を見てきましたが、本章では、動詞、形容詞、副詞をつくる接尾辞、そして形容詞・副詞の比較級と最上級をつくる接尾辞を見ていきましょう。接尾辞は語根にそのままつければいいというものではありません。語根の語尾によって、文字が脱落したり、文字を重ねたりする必要があります。単語を正しく綴るためには、その変化のルールも覚えておく必要があります。

Verbs

A verb is a word that shows action (*run*, *walk*, *fly*, *build*, *have*) or that shows a state of being (*seem*, *be*, *become*). By adding the suffixes *-ate, -en, -ite,* and *-ize* to certain word roots, you create verbs. Here are a few examples:

activ*ate* (to make active)
mut*ate* (to change)
light*en* (to make lighter)
fatt*en* (to make fatter)
un*ite* (to bring together)
demon*ize* (to make into a demon)
ritual*ize* (to make a ritual of)

make X into Y　XをY にする（仕立てる）
demon　悪魔
ritual　儀式

descriptive　説明的な
modify　修飾する

Adjectives

An adjective is any descriptive word that modifies a

noun or a pronoun. (Pronouns are words, *like he, she, they, I* and *them*, that take the place of nouns.) Adjectives can come before the words they modify (the *tall* house), or they can follow the word they modify (the house is *tall*). Certain suffixes like the following create adjectives when attached to word roots:

- *-ful: thoughtful* (contemplative), *wasteful* (using more than is necessary), *purposeful* (aimed at a specific goal), *meaningful* (having significance or purpose), *bountiful* (plentiful)

As the suffix itself implies, its meaning is essentially "full of." So the words literally mean "full of thought," "full of waste," "full of purpose," "full of meaning," and "full of bounty."

- *-less: armless* (without arms), *bloomless* (without blooms), *boundless* (without end), *loveless* (without love), *meatless* (without meat)

Basically the suffix *-less* means without" or "lacking."

- *-able/ible:* acceptable (satisfactory or adequate), *negotiable* (open to discussion), *horrible* (terrible or frightful), *convertible* (able to be changed from one form to another), *invincible* (unbeatable), *infallible* (incapable of error), *unalterable* (permanent)

The suffix *-able/ible* means "capable of," "able to be," or "causing." Therefore, the literal definitions for the preceding words would be "able to be accepted," "able to be negotiated," "causing horror," "able to be converted," and so on.

- ***-y:*** *tricky* (deceitful), *risky* (hazardous), *windy* (accompanied by wind)

The suffix *-y* means "having the characteristics of [the noun that precedes it]."

Adverbs

Adverbs are words that change or explain verbs (ran *quickly*), adjectives (*very* warm), or other adverbs (*too* quickly). Adverbs also indicate when an action happened or will happen (*Tomorrow*, we go to school). Adverbs basically answer the following questions: How? How much? When? The suffix that almost always makes an adverb is *-ly: smartly, happily, warmly*, and *totally* are all examples of adverbs that use *-ly*.

Comparing

If you have things that you want to rank, you need to be able to show degree. Of those things, which is small? Which is smaller? And which is the smallest? Or which is large? Which is larger? And which is the largest?

To show degree, you use the comparative suffixes *-er* and *-est* for most one-syllable and some two-syllable words.

- ***-er:*** You use ***-er*** when you're comparing two things.

Chapter 10

- *-est:* You use *-est* when you're comparing more than two things.

Not all English words loan themselves to these suffixes. Long words, for instance, don't use them (use *more beautiful* instead of beautifuler). Some words, like *good* and *bad,* don't follow the pattern either. The degrees for *bad* are *worse* and *worst*; the degrees for *good* are *better* and *best*.

How Do You Spell That?

Sadly, adding a suffix to a word isn't always as simple as sticking the suffix on at the end of the word. If you did that, you'd end up with quite a few spelling mistakes. To help you stay away from these mistakes, I've added a couple of spelling tips on adding suffixes. Keep in mind, though, that we're talking about the English language.

If the word ends in *-y*, change the *y* to an *i* and add the suffix—if it gives you two *i*'s in a row, then leave the *y*.

> *fancy → fanciful/fancied/fancying*
> *happy → happily/happiness*
> *supply → supplying*
> *whimsy → whimsical*

Whether you add *-d* or *-ed* to a word depends on the end of the word. If the word ends with an *-e*, you generally just add the *-d*. If it ends with another vowel, you add *-ed* (if the word ends in *-y*, remember to change the *y* to an *i*).

in a row　連続して、列をなして

fancy　空想する、〜したい気がする

whimsy　奇行、きまぐれ

Chapter 10

    candy → *candied*
    charge → *charged*
    halo → *haloed*
    hate → *hated*
5   *walk* → *walked*
    tree → *treed* (to force up a tree)

If the word has one syllable and ends in a consonant, you generally repeat the consonant and add the suffix as in:

10 *bat* → *batted*
    if → *iffy* (uncertain)
    wed → *wedding*

Should you use *-ible* or *-able*? Do you add an *-e* or remove an *-e* before you add certain suffixes like
15 *-ment, -ence,* and *-ity*? When do you use *-tion*, and when should it be *-sion*? When you're stumped—or want to be sure you spelled the word right—head to a dictionary.

---

candy　砂糖漬けにして煮る、砂糖をまぶす、甘くする

halo　（光背・光の輪で）囲む

tree　（小動物を）木に追い上げる、追い込む

bat　バットで打つ

iffy　仮定の多い、不確実な
wed　結婚（する）

stumped　途方に暮れる、困る

Exercise

What is the part of speech of the word ending with the following suffixes?

1. -ate: _____
2. -ly: _____
3. -ful: _____
4. -able: _____
5. -ize: _____
6. -less: _____
7. -en: _____
8. -ite: _____

Chapter 11
Homonyms

これまで「語彙力アップの秘密」その1、その2、その3として、接頭辞、語根、接尾辞を詳しく見てきました。つまり、1つの単語を構成するためのパーツを知ることで、単語数を増やす方法を学んできたわけです。本章からは単語数を増やすためのその他の方策を紹介していきます。まずは同音異義語です。同音異義語は綴りと発音が同じで意味が異なる単語を指します。綴りが異なっていて発音が同じであり、意味が異なる単語は異綴同音異義語と言います。巻末には主な同音異義語の一覧を収録してありますのでぜひ活用してください。

Homonyms and Homophones

You may have come across (or may soon run into) words that sound alike but mean different things. These words, named **homonyms** (words with the same spelling and sound) and **homophones** (words with the same pronunciation), are just another hurdle to students trying to learn or improve their use of the English language.

homonym　同音異義語

homophone　異綴同音異義語

Homophones are just words that sound alike, regardless of their spelling and meaning. Examples of homophones include:

awl and *all*
piece and *peace*
to, *two* and *too*
pie and *pi*

awl　ふくろう

pi　ギリシャ文字π、円周率

Chapter 11

Homonyms are words that are spelled the same and sound the same but have different meanings. Some examples of homonyms are:

ball (the toy) and *ball* (the dance)
fine (as in Naoko is one fine-looking woman) and *fine* (the money you pay when you get a parking ticket)
pool (the game), *pool* (the swimming hole) and *pool* (to gather together)
saw (past tense of see) and *saw* (a blade for cutting)

As you go through this section, think about homophones and homonyms and you will find the information to be interesting in a puzzling way.

- All homonyms are also homophones because they sound alike (and that's what makes a homophone a homophone). But not all homophones are homonyms. To be a homonym, the words have to be spelled alike.

- Some words fall into both categories: *Course* and *coarse*, for example, are homophones of each other (they sound alike but are spelled differently). *Course* and *coarse* are also homonyms because each spelling has various meanings.

√ *Coarse* (rough) and *coarse* (vulgar, crude)
- That cloth is so *coarse* (rough) that it scratches her skin.
- What a *coarse* (obscene) film! It cannot be shown to minors.

√ *Course* (direction), *course* (series/trend), and *course* (track)
 - Which *course* (direction) shall we take?
 - The *course* (series) of lectures looks interesting.
 - The golf *course* (track) is so crowded we'll never get on the green.
(*Course* also has some less-often used meanings. You can find them in a dictionary.)

Using Homonyms and Homophones

Homonyms and homophones are like natural disasters. You might get plenty of warning, but you can't escape them. So how do you deal with homonyms? There are no rules that control the use of homonyms; there are only a few memory tricks that help tell apart between them. The few memory tricks that I share here are really only helpful if you're writing and need to know which spelling is correct. For example:

√ *Stationary* has an *a* as in *stay* and means "staying in place;" *Stationery* has an *e* as in *letter* and means "letter-writing paper."
√ *Principal* is a person and ends in *pal*; *principle* is a rule and ends in *-le*.

Although this knowledge is helpful when you write, (when you need to know how to spell a word), it doesn't help you when you're listening. You need to use **context** (text close by a word or passage) to find out what the person you're listening to is talking about—that's about all the strategy you have to use with all homonyms. There is more on **context** and

spelling further on in this book.

So my advice to you is, if possible, to simply learn by heart the meanings and spellings of the words. That way, you can right away recognize the words that are necessary for helping you say what you mean. If you're not sure about a word's meaning or use, check a dictionary to make sure that you pick the word that you want and not its bad twin. Here is a short list of troublesome homonyms and homophones:

Table 11-1 Common and Troublesome Homonyms and Homophones

Word	Meaning	Examples and Notes
aid	(v) to help	She offered *aid* to the victims of the accident.
aide	(n) an assistant	The senator consulted his *aide*.
air	(n) atmosphere	The *air* is clear in the mountains.
heir	(n) one who inherits	He married the *heir* to the crown.
err	(v) to make a mistake	Everyone *errs* at times. *Note: Although *err* is properly pronounced "er," many people pronounce it as "ayr."
all together	(adv) all at one time	We sang the song *all together* very loud.
altogether	(adv) completely or thoroughly	This suit is *altogether* too expensive for my budget.
already	(adv) previously	I've *already* seen that show.
all ready	(adj) completely prepared	Naoko is *all ready* to go to school.
bare	(adj) naked, without covering	He was *bare* when he walked into the room.
bear	(n) a large heavy animal (v) to give birth; to put up with; to carry or hold	Do not feed the *bears*. I *bear* no grudge towards anybody. He had to *bear* the insults at work.
base	(n) foundation for something	Christians *base* their beliefs in the Bible and God.

Chapter 11

bass	(n) low singing voice, a musical instrument, a type of fish	He plays *bass* in the group. I caught a *bass* fishing. *Note: Bass* (a musical instrument) is pronounced the same as *base*. However, *bass* (a fish) is pronounced "*bas*" which rhymes with *glass*.
board	(n) a group of directors, a piece of wood	The *board* of directors decided to fire her.
bored	(adj) weary and disinterested	No matter what, the students were *bored* by the topic of the lecture.
born	(v) brought forth by birth	I was *born* on the seventh of November.
borne	(v) endured (past participle of "to bear")	Yoshitaka had borne the trouble as long as he could before buying a dictionary.
compliment	(n) something said in praise or admiration	He *complimented* her on a job well done.
complement	(n) a complete set of something (v) to make complete	This piece *complements* my model car collection
council	(n) a group of people chosen as an administrative, advisory or legislative assembly.	The *council* made a mistake by hiring that company
counsel	(n) advice, (v) to give advice	Never depend on free *counsel* from a lawyer.
flee	(v) to run away	The children tried to flee from the bully.
flea	(n) a small parasite usually bloodsucking	That dog has *fleas*; it needs to be treated by a vet
fare	(n) the price charged for public transportation	How much is the train *fare* to Shibuya from Ikebukuro?
fair	(adj) not biased (n) a carnival or festival	Judges are supposed to be *fair* in their decisions. I love a good *fair*.
forward	(adv) ahead, toward the future	I always look *forward* to the future.

Chapter 11

foreword	(n) introductory statement in a book	My friend wrote a nice *foreword* in the book.
hear	(v) to perceive sound	The music was so loud that we couldn't *hear* each other.
here	(adv) in this place	The book was *here* a minute ago.
lesson	(n) something to be learned	The teacher taught an interesting lesson.
lessen	(v) to reduce	You have to *lessen* the load on that horse.
maid	(n) a female servant	She needs another *maid* because her house is so big.
made	(v) past tense of "to make"	Everything is made in China nowadays.
mail	(n) letters and packages	They delivered the *mail* to the wrong address.
male	(v) to send via the postal system (adj) man	Do you want a male or a female dog?
pail	(n) bucket	We need a metal pail, not a plastic one.
pale	(adj) ashen, white	His face went *pale* when he saw her.
plait	(n) braid, ribbon (v) to braid	She wears her hair *plaited* into braids.
plate	(n) a dish	You should wash the *plates* and spoons first.
peace	(n) calm, quiet, tranquility, time of no wars	John Lennon wrote and sang "Give *Peace* a Chance."
piece	(n) part of a whole	Would you like a *piece* of cake?
plain	(adj) obvious, not good-looking, (n) an area of level country	It's *plain* you don't know the answer. The Great *Plains* is in America.
plane	(n) carpenter tool used to smooth or to level a wooden surface; an airplane	You need a *plane* to smooth that uneven door. He flies a *plane* on the weekends for fun.

rote	(n) a fixed, mechanical way of doing something	*Rote* repetition is not good for students.
wrote	(v) past tense of write	I *wrote* last night and I will write tonight.
sweet	(adj) delightful or good	A little honey makes my coffee *sweet*.
suite	(n) group of connecting rooms; a set of matched furniture	Ok, I'll get a *suite* in a hotel for the party.
sole	(adj) alone	He was the *sole* customer in the restaurant.
	(n) the bottom of a shoe	The *soles* of my shoes will need replacing soon.
soul	(n) spiritual or emotional force	Where does the *soul* go after one dies?
seed	(n) the source of something	If we plant the *seeds* here they will grow.
cede	(v) to give up	The enemy *ceded* the battle and retreated.
sight	(n) vision	He lost his *sight* in childhood.
cite	(v) to quote	He *cited* Shakespeare on his paper.
site	(n) location or place	Gaijinpot.com is a *site* on the internet
throne	(n) king's or queen's chair	The king's *throne* was magnificent.
thrown	(v) past participle of "to throw"	Naoko had *thrown* the book in anger!
tail	(n) rear limb on an animal	A dog wags his *tail* when he likes someone.
	(v) to follow	You have to *tail* him to find out what he's doing.
tale	(n) story	She told a tall *tale* to her parents but they did not believe it.

Exercise

Answer these 6 questions.

1. What is a homonym?
2. What is a homophone?
3. Why are all homonyms also homophones?
4. Why are all homophones not homonyms?
5. Give example of words that fall into both categories.
6. What should you do if you're not sure about a word's meaning or use?

Chapter 12
Compounding Words

単語と単語を組み合わせると新しい単語が生まれます。この新しい単語を複合語と呼びます。複合語には、1語として綴るもの、2語あるいは3語のもの、あるいはハイフンで結ばれたものなど、表記法の異なるものがあります。本章ではこれらの複合語について見ていきます。接頭辞＋語根＋接尾辞と、単語＋単語はどう違うのでしょうか。その答えは本文に書いてあります。複合語の作り方を覚えておけば、何かを表現したい時、正しい単語を知らなくても、すでに知っている単語を組み合わせて表現することも可能になります。

Compound Basics

One way to explain something new is to unite two words to form a new word. The combination gives the new word a particular meaning that is kilometers apart from the unique meaning of the unconnected words. For example, you bring together "head" and "line" to get "headline." A headline is the title of a piece of writing in a newspaper or magazine, not a line on your head.

Compound words are made up of two or more words written as one word (*newspaper*, for example), a hyphenated word (*father-in-law*), or two or more words that stand for an idea or a single thing (like *Commander in Chief* or *school bus*).

Because compound words turn up in different forms, how can you tell whether a word is really a compound word or just a compound wannabe? There are two

～wannabe ～になりたがっている者、XX予備軍

simple courses of action to help you figure out if a word is a true compound:

√ **Each element must be a complete word.** *Pre-law* is not a compound word because *pre-* is not a complete word (even though *law* is). *Goldfish*, however, is a compound word because *gold* and *fish* are separate words.

√ **No letters are dropped or added when the compound word is formed.** When a prefix or suffix is added to a word, letters are often dropped (removed) or added. Similarly, when two distinct words come together, letters are often dropped or changed in order to join the words. A compound word, however, is formed by just putting the two words together without adding or removing any letters to do so.

Compound word:
   with + out = without
   day + light = daylight
Not a compound word:
   holy + day = holiday

Compound word:
   like + able = likeable
Not a compound word:
   justify + able = justifiable

Closed Compounds

Closed compounds turn up as one word with no break between the words used to make it. In addition, no letters are added or removed in order to make the compound; the two words are just put together. As in any compound word, you can use the meaning of the specific words to figure out the meaning of the compound. As you read the examples in the table that follow, cover the "Definition" section. Knowing each part of the compound word can help you understand the new word it forms.

Table 12–1 Closed Compound Words

Word + Word	= Compound	Definition
book + case	bookcase	cabinet for books
cross + road	crossroads	where two roads cross
house + fly	housefly	a fly that lives in and around a house
rain + coat	raincoat	a coat that repels rain
steam + boat	steamboat	a boat powered by steam
window + sill	windowsill	ledge of a window
with + out	without	lacking, not having
any + one	anyone	any person, anybody

You can make a lot of compound words with the word *super*. Most of these words use *super* as a prefix, as in *superabundant* (very abundant), *superhuman* (more than human), and *supercharge* (charge with an unnecessary amount). However, a handful of compound words use *super* as a word rather than a prefix. For example, we have *superannuate* which means "to allow to retire on a pension because of age or sickness.

Hyphenated Compounds

Hyphenated compounds are written as one-word—two words joined by a hyphen.

Table 12–2 Hyphenated Compound Words		
Word + Word	**= Compound**	**Definition**
able + bodied	able-bodied	fit, healthy
bell + like	bell-like	like a bell
cross + examine	cross-examine	question in court
great + grandfather	great-grandfather	relative
old + fashioned	old-fashioned	traditional

Although many hyphenated compounds are built from two words, as the table above shows, you can also find quite a few common three-word compounds: *father-in-law* (and the other *in-law* words), *five-year-old*, and *show-and-tell*, for instance.

It is often hard to determine whether a word is hyphenated. Sometimes the hyphen depends on what part of speech the word is. For example, *show-off* is hyphenated as a noun but not as a verb (*show off*). To add to the confusion, you can't always depend on similar words being treated the same way. For example, you hyphenate *brother-in-law, mother-in-law,* and the other *in-law* words, but you don't hyphenate *commander in chief*. The following rules usually work:

√ **Use a hyphen in compound words beginning with self:** *self-satisfied, self-examine*, and so on.
√ **Use a hyphen in compound words that end with elect:** *president-elect*

When you apply the preceding rules, be sure that you're combing two complete words—not a root and a suffix or prefix that aren't words themselves. For example, *self-examine, self-elect, self-respect* are hyphenated compounds. *Selfishness* and *reelect* aren't compound words and therefore don't use hyphens. (But you can choose to hyphenate *re-elect* just to distinguish between the double *e*.)

√**You usually hyphenate compound words that begin with** *all (all-around and all-American)*. Keep in mind, though, that this isn't always the case (*all in one*).

√**Use an up-to-date dictionary.** If you are not sure whether a word should be hyphenated, look it up.

No matter how a compound is written, you can still use the individual words to get an idea of the compound word's meaning. Often, the meaning of the compound is a sort of combination of the meanings of these individual words. For example, *shuffleboard* (the game in which you use long cues to shove disks along a smooth surface) is made up of the word *shuffle* (a dragging, sliding movement) and the word *board* (a flat surface, usually made of wood).

shove 〜を押して前へ進める

drag 引きずる

1. **Write down unfamiliar compound words that you hear or read.**
2. **Look the word up in the dictionary to find out whether it's a closed compound, hyphenated compound, or open compound.**
3. **Group related words.**

For example, put all the words about the sun together. Doing this makes it easier for you to see how the words are similar.

Chapter 12

Exercise

Answer the following questions.

1. How are compound words made up?
2. How can you tell whether a word is really a compound word?
3. In what two ways do closed compounds turn up?
4. How are hyphenated compounds written?
5. Why is it often hard to determine whether a word is hyphenated?

Chapter 13
Synonyms, Antonyms, and Clipped Words

英語では、同じ単語や表現を繰り返さないのがよい文章だと考えられています。そのため、1つのものを表現するのに次々と類義語で置き換えていくのです。また、反意語も表現のバリエーションを増やす方法の1つです。反意語を否定することで同じ意味をあらわすことができるからです。1つの単語を覚えるときには、その類義語や反意語も一緒に覚えるようにしましょう。ただし、覚える際には語法や使用可能な場面などが異なる場合もあるので注意が必要です。

Synonyms

Synonyms are different words with identical or very similar meanings. Words that are synonyms are said to be **synonymous**, and the state of being a synonym
5　is called **synonymy**. The word comes from Ancient Greek *syn* (with) and *onoma* (name). The words *car* and *automobile* are synonyms. Similarly, if we talk about a long time or an extended time, *long* and *extended* become synonyms. In the figurative sense,
10　two words are often said to be synonymous if they have the same connotation.

Synonyms can be any part of speech (e.g. nouns, verbs, adjectives, adverbs or prepositions), as long as both members of the pair are the same part of speech.
15　More examples of English synonyms are:

identical　まったく同じ、等しい

figurative　比ゆ的な

connotation　暗示的意味、含み

Chapter 13

baby and *infant* (noun)
petty crime and *misdemeanor* (noun)
student and *pupil* (noun)
buy and *purchase* (verb)
5   *pretty* and *attractive* (adjective)
sick and *ill* (adjective)
quickly and *speedily* (adverb)
on and *upon* (preposition)
freedom and *liberty* (noun)
10   *dead* and *deceased* (adjective)
cop and *police officer* (noun)
movie and *film* (noun)

*Note: that the synonyms are defined with respect to certain senses of words; for instance,
15   *pupil* as the "aperture in the iris of the eye" is not synonymous with *student*. Similarly, *expired* as "having lost validity" (as in grocery goods) doesn't necessarily mean *death*.

In English many synonyms evolved from a mixture
20   of Norman French and English words, often with some words associated with the Saxon countryside (*folk*, *freedom*) being synonymous with the Norman nobility (*people*, *liberty*).

Some people claim that no synonyms have exactly
25   the same meaning (in all contexts or social levels of language) because etymology, orthography, phonic qualities, ambiguous meanings, usage, etc. make them unique. Different words that are similar in meaning usually differ for a reason: *feline* is more
30   formal than *cat*; *long* and *extended* are only syn-

---

petty crime / misdemeanor 軽犯罪

pupil 瞳（孔）
aperture 開口部、(レンズの）口径

etymology 語源学
orthography 正書法
ambiguous あいまいな、両義にとれる

onyms in one usage and not in others (for example, a *long* arm is not the same as an *extended* arm). Synonyms are also a source of inoffensive words.

The use of a human natural language is a matter of agreement between people and names of things (words) are arbitrarily given to objects. Such names are meant to identify things, etc. and are therefore unique identifiers at the start, though may be longer than a single word. So what you have is a list of words that may replace each other subject to various contextual circumstances.

Antonyms (Gradable Opposites)

Antonyms, from the Greek *anti* ("opposite") and *onoma* ("name") are word pairs that are opposite in meaning, such as *hot* and *cold*, *fat* and *skinny*, and *up* and *down*. Words may have different antonyms, depending on the meaning. Both *long* and *tall* are antonyms of *short*. Gradable opposites are two ends of the spectrum (*slow* and *fast*) but can have variations in between.

The term antonym (and the related antonymy) has also been commonly used as a term that is synonymous with opposite; however, the term also has other more restricted meanings. One usage has antonym referring to both gradable opposites, such as *long-short*, and (non-gradable) complementary opposites, such as *male-female*, while opposites of the types *up-down* and *precede-follow* are excluded from the definition. A third usage defines the term antonym as referring to only gradable opposites (the *long-short* type) while the other types are referred to with different terms.

Relational antonyms (converses) are pairs in which one describes a relationship between two objects and the other describes the same relationship when the two objects are reversed, such as *parent* and *child*, *teacher* and *student*, or *buy* and *sell*.

relational antonym 関係的反意語

Contranym

Contranyms (also called auto-antonyms) are the same words that can mean the opposite of themselves under different contexts or having separate definitions.

contranym コントロニム (元の綴りは contronym であった)

enjoin:	a.	to prohibit, issue injunction
	b.	to order, command
fast:	a.	moving quickly
	b.	fixed firmly in place
cleave:	a.	to split
	b.	to adhere
sanction:	a.	punishment, prohibition
	b.	permission
stay:	a.	remain in a specific place, postpone
	b.	guide direction, movement

injunction 禁止命令
command 命令

adhere 付着する

Clipped Words

Some nonnative speakers choose to write the clipped form of some words. A clipped word is a word shortened by common use. Clipped words are favored because they are easier to spell. The challenge occurs when students are asked to write the longer form of a clipped word. Some common clipped words are listed

clipped word 略語

below.

Table 13–1 Common Clipped Words			
Clipped Word	**Longer Form**	**Clipped Word**	**Longer Form**
ad	advertisement	memo	memorandum
auto	automobile	mike	microphone
bike	bicycle	mum	chrysanthemum
burger	hamburger	pen	penitentiary
bus	omnibus	phone	telephone
champ	champion	photo	photograph
con	convict	pike	turnpike
co-op	cooperative	plane	airplane
copter	helicopter	ref	referee
cuke	cucumber	rev	revolution
dorm	dormitory	rhino	rhinoceros
exam	examination	specs	spectacles; specifications
flu	influenza	stats	statistics
fridge	refrigerator	stereo	stereophonics
gas	gasoline	sub	submarine
grad	graduate	taxi	taxicab
gym	gymnasium	teen	teenager
hippo	hippopotamus	tie	necktie
lab	laboratory	tux	tuxedo
limo	limousine	typo	typographical error
lunch	luncheon	van	caravan
math	mathematics	vet	veteran; veterinarian

Contractions

A contraction is a word made from a verb and another word. An apostrophe takes the place of any letters
5　that are left out. A contraction can be made by joining a verb and the word *not*, a word and the verb *is*, and a pronoun and a verb. Here are some common contrac-

contraction　縮約形

Chapter 13

tions that students should know how to spell.

Table 13–2 Common Contractions: Verb + Not			
aren't	are not	haven't	have not
can't	cannot	isn't	is not
couldn't	could not	mustn't	must not
didn't	did not	shouldn't	should not
doesn't	does not	wasn't	was not
don't	do not	weren't	were not
hadn't	had not	won't	will not
hasn't	has not	wouldn't	would not

Table 13–3 Common Contractions: Word + Is			
here's	here is	what's	what is
that's	that is	where's	where is
there's	there is	who's	who is

Table 13–4 Common Contractions: Pronoun + Verb			
he'd	he would, he had	they'll	they will
I'd	I would, I had	they're	they are
I'll	I will	they've	they have
I'm	I am	we'd	we would, we had
I've	I have	we'll	we will
it'll	it will	we're	we are
it's	it is, it has	we've	we have
she'd	she would, she had	who'll	who will
she'll	she will	you'd	you would, you had
she's	she is, she has	you'll	you will
they'd	they would, they had	you're	you are

Sometimes the contractions *he'll, I'll, it's, there's, they're, we'd, we've, who's,* and *you're* are confused with other words that sound the same (*heal/heel,*

Chapter 13

aisle/isle, its, theirs, their/there, weed, weave, whose, your). Students must understand the different spellings and meanings of these words with the same sounds.

Exercise

Answer the questions in complete sentences.

1. What are synonyms?
2. How can synonyms be any part of speech?
3. How did many synonyms evolved in English?
4. What are antonyms?
5. What is a clipped word?
6. What is a contraction?

Chapter 14
Articles

本章では、英語学習者がつまずきやすいポイントにスポットを当てます。その1つが冠詞です。a と an の使い分けの決まりは理解していますか？ a/an と the の使い分けはいかがですか？ 冠詞の使い方と関係してくるのが可算名詞と不可算名詞の区別です。これは日本語にはない区別なので、名詞を覚えるときにはいちいち可算か不可算かということを意識する必要があります。そのほか、比較級、固有名詞、関係代名詞の who と which と that なども取り上げます。

A or An

When English is your second language, you face the special challenges of learning characteristics of English that native-born speakers take for granted. Here are ten ways to help you deal with some of the most baffling problems that English vocabulary can pose for people learning it as a second language.

Often, it's the little words rather than the big ones that trip up second-language speakers. *A* and *an* are small but crucial words. Although both *a* and *an* refer to a singular person, place or thing, *a* is used before words that begin with a consonant sound, and *an* is used before words that begin with a vowel sound. Remember that the vowels are *a, e, i, o, u,* and sometimes *y;* the consonants are all the other letters in the alphabet. However, it's not enough to identify vowels and consonants, because their sounds can be created by other letters, as the following shows:

baffling 困惑させる、厄介な
pose （問題などを）引き起こす、提起する

trip up （人を）つまづかせる、（人の）揚げ足をとる

Table 14–1 Consonant and Vowel Sounds	
Words with Consonant Sounds	**Words with Vowel Sounds**
a history lesson ("h" sound)	an honest man (no "h" sound)
a one-horse town ("w" sound)	an only child ("o" sound)

Check out the "*The and A*" section further along this chapter for more tips on how to use these articles.

Degree of Comparison

Adjectives and adverbs, words used to describe things or actions, have different forms to show *degree* (or amount) of comparison:

- √ The *positive* degree is the basic form of the word without any comparison being made.
- √ The *comparative* degree is used to compare two things. Often, these words end in *-er* or use *more*, but never both.
- √ The *superlative* degree is used to compare three or more things. Often, these words end in *-est*, or use *most*, but never both.

To see how degrees of comparison work, consider these examples: *fast* (positive), *faster* (comparative), *fastest* (superlative), *quickly* (positive), *more quickly* (comparative), and *most quickly* (superlative).

Some adjectives do not follow this pattern. The following words pose special challenge for nonnative speakers.

Table 14–2 Comparatives & Superlatives of Adjectives		
Positive	Comparative	Superlative
good	better (not gooder)	best (not goodest)
bad	worse (not badder)	worst (not baddest)
late	later	last or latest

These usage tips may also be helpful:

- √ Use *more* and *most* to form the comparative and superlative degrees of all modifiers (word qualifying another) with three or more syllables. For example: *more popular, most popular, more affectionate, most affectionate*.
- √ Don't use *more* and *-er* together to form a comparative (*more happier*, for example). Similarly, don't use most and *-est* together to form a superlative (*most nicest*, for example).
- √ Use the comparative degree when you're comparing two things. For example; of the two sisters, the *younger* one is smarter. Use the superlative degree when you're comparing three or more things. For example; of the seven children, he is the *youngest*.

Count Nouns

Some English nouns name items that can be counted, such as *newspaper, street* and *idea*. You say "I have a newspaper" or "I have a hundred newspapers from the past year," for example. In other words count nouns are plural or singular nouns that indicate number.

Chapter 14

Non-count Nouns

English has other nouns that identify objects thought of as a whole. Therefore, these objects are not divided into separate parts that can be counted. Examples include *sand, blood, beef, salt, sugar, rice, traffic, water* and *coffee*. These words are never preceded by *a* or *an* and are never plural.

Table 14–4 Non-count Nouns	
Category	Examples
abstract ideas	advice, equality, health, fun, information, news, peace, respect
food	bread, butter, pork, cheese
gases	air, helium, hydrogen
languages	Japanese, Chinese, Korean, Spanish
liquids	coffee, gasoline, water, tea, milk
pastimes	chess, homework, housework, soccer
things	clothing, furniture, jewelry, luggage, money, mail, vocabulary

Nouns That Can Be Both Count and Non-count

Some nouns can be count nouns and non-count nouns, depending on the way you use them in your speech or writing. If the noun names something that can be taken individually or as a whole, it can be used both ways. For example:

Count: You have a *hair* on your shoulder.
Non-count: Masami has black *hair*

Nouns as Adjectives

Adjectives are words that describe a noun or pronoun. It sounds easy enough, but in English, words are used as different parts of speech all the time. Sometimes a word is a noun and sometimes it's an adjective. Consider this sentence, for example:

We went to the train station to ride a train.

Train is used twice in this sentence, once as an adjective and once as a noun. How do you tell the difference? You use the context: The first *train* is an adjective because it describes the kind of station. The second *train* in the sentence is a noun.

Adjectives do not have plural forms. When you use an adjective with a plural noun, don't make the adjective plural. For example: the *train* (not *trains*) stations and the *yellow* (not *yellows*) flowers.

Plurals

Many nouns form regular plurals (more than one) by adding *-s* or *-es*, as in *coat/coats*, or *fox/foxes*. Nouns whose singular ends in *-y* normally form their plural by changing *-y* to *-ies*; one *city*, two *cities*. Other nouns have irregular plurals, which means that making their plural isn't as simple as adding *-s* or *-es*. Examples of irregular plural include *foot/feet*, and *leaf/leaves*.

If you're not sure whether a noun is plural, look it up in a dictionary. If no plural is given for a singular noun, add *-s/-es* to form the plural.

Proper Nouns

Proper nouns name specific people, places, or things. For example: *Mexico, Emperor Showa, Jell-O.*

Always capitalize proper nouns. Most proper nouns do not need an article (a, an, the). For example; We visited (not *the*) Mt. Fuji. There are several exceptions, however, such as *the Rocky Mountains, the Great Lakes*, and *the Amazon*.

The and A

The and *a* or *an* precede nouns: the house, a horse, an apple, for example. Which one you use depends on whether you are referring to a specific thing or a nonspecific thing.

- √ Use *the* to refer to a specific person, place, or thing. For example: *the* soccer game (one specific game), *the* sari (one specific sari), and *the* hamburger (one specific hamburger)
- √ Use *a* or *an* to indicate any item in a group. For example: *a* kitten (not any particular kitten), or *an* apple (any apple).

Who, Which, That

Who refers only to people:
   He is the man *who* delivered the package.

Which refers only to things:
   The package **which** I received yesterday was not from him.

That refers to both people and things:
   The package *that* I found on the table came from my aunt *that* lives in the West Coast.

Chapter 14

Exercise

Answer true or false.

1. How is the word *a* used?
2. How is the word *an* used?
3. What are count nouns?
4. What are non-count nouns?
5. What are proper nouns?

Chapter 15
Knowledge is Reading

前章までは接頭辞、語根、接尾辞のほか、同意語、反意語など単語に関する知識を深めてきました。ここからは単語を増やすのに有効な手段であるリーディングについて学んでいきます。これが「語彙力アップの秘密」その4です。語彙力だけでなく、英語力全般を強化したいのであれば、やはり多読が必要です。ただ、たくさん読むと言っても、やみくもに読み始めて挫折してしまっては意味がありません。本章では、効果的に読むための6つの"戦略"を紹介します。6つの"戦略"で準備が整ったら、お好きな素材で多読をスタートしてください。

Here Is Secret #4

Secrets one, two, and three gave you the knowledge that comes from understanding the meanings of prefixes, roots, and suffixes and how they work to make them work for you. But knowing this alone is not enough; you have to put this knowledge into practice by reading. You should read English as often and as much as you can. Reading will greatly help you to increase your vocabulary now that you understand secrets 1–3. Reading will help your pronunciation, grammar, and finally your conversation. How? As your vocabulary increases, you have more words to use in a conversation. When taking a test your scores will be higher! Why? Because now you have a better understanding of the words of what you read.

Motivation Is Necessary

Without setting the time for reading, no one can gain

Chapter 15

the reading skills or knowledge they need to succeed in school, at work, or in life in general. The best way to improve your reading efficiency is to read a lot. "I don't have the time." How? When riding the trains to
5 school or work, read. During lunchtime, read; instead of watching television for three hours, set one hour aside for reading. Read books or magazines about things that interest you, not what interests your teacher.

10 ## 6 Reading Strategies

strategy 戦略

Good reading strategies help you to read in a very effective way. Using them, you aim to get the maximum benefit from your reading with the minimum effort. Here I will show you how to use six different
15 strategies to read intelligently.

Strategy 1: Knowing what you want to know
The first thing to ask yourself is: Why you are reading the text? Are you reading with a purpose or just for pleasure? What do you want to know after reading it?

20 Once you know this, you can examine the text to see whether it is going to move you towards this goal.

An easy way of doing this is to look at the introduction and the chapter headings. The introduction should let you know whom the book is targeted at,
25 and what it seeks to achieve. Chapter headings will give you an overall view of the structure of the subject.

Ask yourself whether the book meets your needs. Ask

yourself if it assumes too much or too little knowledge. If the book isn't ideal, would it be better to find a better one?

Strategy 2: Knowing how deeply to study the material

Where you only need the shallowest knowledge of the subject, you can *skim* (glance through books or paper) the material. You read only chapter headings, introductions and summaries.

If you need a moderate level of information on a subject, then you can *scan* (read quickly) the text. You read the chapter introductions and summaries in detail. You may then speed-read the contents of the chapters, picking out and understanding key words and concepts. At this level of looking at the document it is worth paying attention to diagrams and graphs.

Only when you need detailed knowledge of a subject is it worth studying the text. Here it is best to *skim* the material first to get an overview of the subject. This gives you an understanding of its structure, into which you can fit the detail gained from a full, receptive reading of the material.

Strategy 3: Active Reading

When you are reading a document in detail, it often helps if you highlight, underline and take notes as you go on. This calls attention to information in your mind, and helps you to review important points later.

Doing this also helps to keep your mind focused on the material and stops it wandering.

Strategy 4: How to study different sorts of material

Different sorts of documents hold information in different places and in different ways. They have different depths and breadths of coverage. By understanding the layout of the material you are reading, you can dig out useful information much more efficiently.

• Reading Magazines and Newspapers

These tend to give a very disjointed coverage of an area. They will typically only concentrate on the most interesting and glamorous parts of a topic—this helps them to sell copies! They will often ignore less interesting information that may be important to a full understanding of a subject.

The most effective way of getting information from magazines is to scan the contents tables or indexes and turn directly to interesting articles. If you find an article useful, then cut it out and file it in a folder specifically covering that sort of information. In this way you will build up sets of related articles that may begin to explain the subject.

Newspapers tend to be arranged in sections. If you read a paper often, you can learn quickly which sections are useful and which ones you can skip altogether.

---

wander　さまよう、横道にそれる、(思考など)とりとめがなくなる

disjointed　統合されていない、まとまりのない

glamorous　魅惑的な、華やかな

Chapter 15

- **Reading Individual Articles**

Articles within newspapers and magazines tend to be in three main types:

News Articles: Here the most important information is presented first, with information being less and less useful as the article progresses. News articles are designed to explain the key points first, and then flesh them out with detail.

flesh out　肉付けする、具体化する

Opinion Articles: Opinion articles present a point of view. Here the most important information is contained in the introduction and the summary, with the middle of the article containing supporting arguments.

Feature Articles: These are written to provide entertainment or background on a subject. Typically the most important information is in the body of the text.

feature article　特集記事

If you know what you want from an article, and recognize its type, you can extract information from it quickly and efficiently.

extract　抽出する

Strategy 5: Reading 'whole subject' documents

When you are reading an important document, it is easy to accept the writer's arrangement of thought. This can mean that you may not notice that important information has been left out or that irrelevant detail has been included. A good way of recognizing this is to read the table of contents before you open the document. You can then use this table of contents

irrelevant　無関係の、不適切な、重要でない

Chapter 15

to read the document in the order that you want. You will be able to spot omissions quickly.

Strategy 6: Using glossaries with technical documents

If you are reading large amounts of difficult technical material, it may be useful to photocopy or compile a glossary. Keep this beside you as you read. It will probably also be useful to note down the key ideas in your own words, and refer to them when necessary.

Usually it is best to make notes as you go.

omission 省略

glossary 用語集

Exercise

Answer true or false.

1. Why is reading important?
2. What is necessary in reading?
3. How many reading strategies are there? List them.

Chapter 16
The Reading Process

前章では効果的な読み方をするためにどんな準備をすればよいかということを学んできました。本章では、実際に読んでいる最中に気をつけるべきポイントを挙げていきます。20以上の項目をリストアップしてありますが、この中で無理なく続けられそうなものをいくつか試してみてください。better reader になるための道は１つではありません。あなたにとって効果的なリーディング・スタイルをぜひ見つけ出してください。

Strategies of Good Readers

Good readers understand the processes involved in reading and consciously control them. This awareness and control of the reading processes is called **metacognition**, which means "knowing about knowing." Some students don't know when they don't know. They continue to read even though they do not understand. Poor readers put up with such confusion because they either don't realize that it exists or don't know what to do about it. Poor readers focus on facts, whereas good readers try to take in details into a larger reasoning pattern.

Below is a list of reading strategies to try. Keep in mind that any three strategies may be enough to make you a better reader. Experiment with different methods and see what works for you. The goal is to develop your own reading system, which will help you in the long term, not just for class, but for life.

metacognition　メタ認知

put up with 〜　〜に耐える、〜を我慢する

Chapter 16

- Read sitting up, with a good light, at a desk or table.
- Keep background noise to a minimum. Loud rock and roll music will not make you a better reader.
- The same goes for screaming kids, talking roommates, television or radio. Give yourself a quiet environment so that you can concentrate on the text.
- Keep paper and a pen within reach.
- Before beginning to read, think about the purpose for the reading. Why has the teacher made this assignment? What are you supposed to get out of it? Jot down your thoughts.
- Survey the reading. Look at the title of the piece, the subheadings. What is in dark print or stands out? Are there illustrations or graphs?
- Read the introduction and conclusion, then go back and read the whole assignment. Or read the first line in every paragraph to get an idea of how the ideas progress, then go back and read from the beginning.
- Scan the entire reading, then focus on the most interesting or relevant parts to read in detail.
- Pay attention to when you can skim and when you need to understand every word.
- Write as you read. Take notes and talk back to the text. Explicate (explain in detail) and mark up the pages. Write down what interests or bores you. Speculate about why.
- If you get stuck in the reading, think and write about where you got stuck. Contemplate why that particular place was difficult and how you might break through the block.

jot down 走り書きする

speculate 思索する、推測する
get stuck 行き詰る、立ち往生する
comtemplate 熟考する

Chapter 16

- Record and explore your confusion. Confusion is important because it's the first stage in understanding.
- When the going gets difficult, and you don't understand the reading, slow down and reread sections.
- Break long assignments into segments. Read 10 pages, then do something else. Later, read the next 10 pages and so on.
- Read prefaces and summaries to learn important details about the book. Look at the table of contents for information about the structure and movement of ideas. Use the index to look up specific names, places, ideas.
- Translate difficult material into your own words. Create an alternative text.
- Answer the questions at the end of the chapter.
- Answer these questions in your own words: What's the author talking about? What does the author want me to get out of this?
- Read the entire piece, then write a one-paragraph or one-sentence summary.
- Transcribe your notes in the book or handwritten notes into more formal notes on the computer. Turn your first notes into a list of ideas or a short essay.
- Review the ideas in the text after you finish reading. Ask yourself questions to determine what you got out of the reading.
- Mark up the text, bring it to class, and ask questions about what you don't understand.
- Post an email to the class Mailing List and ask for responses from the teacher and fellow students.
- Consult another source. What does another author have to say on the same topic?

transcribe 書き直す、転記する

- Disagree with the author. Become a devil's advocate. Remember, you don't have to believe an idea to argue about it.
- Think about the text in three ways.
  1. Consider the text itself, the basic information right there on the page. (This is the level of most high school readers and many college students.)
  2. Next, think about what is between the lines, the conclusions and inferences the author means you to draw from the text.
  3. Finally, go beyond thinking about the text. What creative, new, and different thoughts occur as you combine your knowledge and experiences with the ideas in the reading?

devil's advocate 「悪魔の代弁者」（わざと反論する人、あら探しをする人）

inference 推論

Reading Rate

"Reading well" does not mean reading everything at the same pace and with the same technique. As a university student, much of your reading will be assigned material. You get information from everything you read and yet you don't read everything for the same reason or in the same way. For example, a novel can be read quickly just to get the story, whereas a poem might be read slowly, perhaps several times to find out the meaning.

Good readers are flexible readers. Once they determine their purpose for reading, they adjust their rate to fit the type of material they are reading.

Five Categories of Reading Rates
- **Careful:** used to master content including details, judge material, outline, summarize, paraphrase,

Chapter 16

analyze, solve problems, memorize, evaluate literary value or read poetry.

- **Normal:** used to answer a specific question, note details, solve problems, read material of average difficulty, understand relationship of details to main ideas, appreciate beauty or literary style, keep up with current events, or read with the intention of later retelling what you have read.
- **Rapid:** used to review familiar material, get the main idea or central thought, retrieve information for short-term use, read light material for relaxation or pleasure or comprehend the basic plot.
- **Scanning:** the method by which you read the newspaper—used to get an overview of the content or to preview.
- **Skimming:** done a little more quickly. It is what you do when you are searching for something particular in the text—the way you might read a phone book or dictionary. Used to find a specific reference, locate new material, locate the answer to a specific question, get the main idea of a selection, or review.

retrieve （情報を）検索する、読み出す

Exercise

Answer true or false.

1. What is *metacognition?*
2. How many categories of reading rate are there, and can you list them?
3. How is "Careful" used as a reading rate?
4. How is "Normal" used as a reading rate?
5. How is "Rapid" used as a reading rate?

Chapter 17
Identifying Topics, Main Ideas, and Supporting Details

詩や小説は別として、何らかの情報を伝えるための英文は非常に明白な構造を持っています。日本語の文章は「起・承・転・結」で構成されますが、英語の文章は Introduction-Body-Conclusion という三段論法でパラグラフを積み上げていきます。個々のパラグラフで述べるのは 1 つの idea のみというルールがあり、それを 1 つの topic sentence と複数の supporting sentence を使って表現していきます。本章では、このような英文パラグラフの構造や種類について学びます。

Concept Framework of a Paragraph

Understanding the **topic**, the **gist**, or the larger concept framework of a textbook chapter, an article, a paragraph, a sentence or a passage is a mature reading task. Being able to draw conclusions, evaluate, and critically interpret articles or chapters is important for overall comprehension in reading. Textbook chapters, articles, paragraphs, sentences, or passages all have topics and main ideas. The **topic** is the broad, general theme or message. It is what some call the **subject**. The **main idea** is the "key concept" being expressed. **Details**, major and minor, support the main idea by telling how, what, when, where, why, how much, or how many. Locating the topic, main idea, and supporting details helps you understand the point(s) the writer is attempting to express. Identifying the rela-

gist 主旨、要点

tionship between these will increase your comprehension.

The successful communication of any author's topic is only as good as the organization the author uses to build and define his/her subject matter.

Understanding the Main Idea

A **paragraph** is a group of sentences related to a particular topic, or central theme. Every paragraph has a key concept or main idea. The main idea is the most important piece of information the author wants you to know about the concept of that paragraph.

When authors write, they have an idea in mind that they are trying to get across. This is especially true as authors create paragraphs. An author organizes each paragraph's main idea and supporting details in support of the topic or central theme, and each paragraph supports the paragraph before it.

A writer will state his/her main idea clearly somewhere in the paragraph. That main idea may be stated at the beginning of the paragraph, in the middle, or at the end. The sentence in which the main idea is stated is called the **topic sentence** of that paragraph.

The topic sentence announces the general theme (or portion of the theme) to be dealt with in the paragraph. Although the topic sentence may appear anywhere in the paragraph, it is usually first—and for a very good reason. This sentence provides the focus for the writer while writing and for the reader while reading. When you find the topic sentence, be sure to underline it so that it will stand out not only now, but also later when you review.

Identifying the Topic

The first thing you must be able to do to get at **the main idea** of a paragraph is to identify **the topic**—the subject of the paragraph. Think of the paragraph as a wheel with the topic being the hub—the central core around which the whole wheel (or paragraph) spins.

Your strategy for topic identification is simply to ask yourself the question, "What is this about?" Keep asking yourself that question as you read a paragraph, until the answer to your question becomes clear. Sometimes you can spot the topic by looking for a word or two that repeat. Usually you can state the topic in a few words.

Let us try this topic-finding strategy. Reread the first paragraph under the heading *Understanding the Main Idea* on the previous page. Ask yourself the question, "What is this paragraph about?" To answer, say to yourself in your mind, "The author keeps talking about paragraphs and the way they are designed. This must be the topic—paragraph organization." Reread the second paragraph of the same section. Ask yourself "What is this paragraph about?" Did you say to yourself, "This paragraph is about different ways to organize a paragraph"? That is the topic. Next, reread the third paragraph and see if you can find the topic of the paragraph. How? Write the topic in the margin next to this paragraph. Remember, getting the main idea of a paragraph is crucial to reading.

hub 車輪・プロペラ等の中心部

Chapter 17

The main part of an **expository paragraph** (a type of paragraph, the purpose of which is to inform, explain, describe, or define the author's subject to the reader) is made up of **supporting sentences** (major and minor details), which help to explain or prove the main idea. These sentences present facts, reasons, examples, definitions, comparison, contrasts, and other relevant details. They are most important because they sell the main idea.

sell 売り込む、納得させる

The last sentence of a paragraph is likely to be **a concluding sentence**. It is used to sum up a discussion, to stress a point, or to restate all or part of the topic sentence so as to bring the paragraph to a close. The last sentence may also be **a transitional** (go-between) **sentence** leading to the next paragraph.

Of course, the paragraphs you'll be reading will be part of some longer piece of writing—a textbook chapter, a section of a chapter, or a newspaper or magazine article. Besides **expository paragraphs**, in which new information is presented and discussed, these longer writings contain three types of paragraphs: **introductory**, **transitional**, and **summarizing**.

- **Introductory paragraphs** tell you, in advance, such things as (1) the main ideas of the chapter or section; (2) the extent or limits of the coverage; (3) how the topic is developed; and (4) the writer's attitude toward the topic.

- **Transitional paragraphs** are usually short; their

sole function is to tie together what you have read so far and what is to come—to set the stage for succeeding ideas of the chapter or section.

- **Summarizing paragraphs** are used to restate briefly the main ideas of the chapter or section. The writer may also draw some conclusion from these ideas, or speculate on some conclusion based on the evidence he/she has presented.

All three types should *alert* you: the introductory paragraph of things to come; the transitional paragraph of a new topic; and the summarizing paragraph of main ideas that you should have gotten.

Exercise

Read the following paragraph and underline the stated main idea. Write down in your own words what you are able to conclude from the information.

The rules of conduct during an examination are clear. No books, calculators or papers are allowed in the test room. Proctors will not allow anyone with such items to take the test. Anyone caught cheating will be asked to leave the room. His or her test sheet will be taken. The incident will be reported to the proper authority. At the end of the test period, all materials will be returned to the proctor. Failure to abide by these rules will result in a failing grade for this test.

Chapter 18
Making Inferences and Drawing Conclusions

リーディングは、個々の文の意味を理解するだけでは事足りません。言葉で書かれていることも書かれていないことも含めて、文章全体として著者が何を伝えたいのかということを理解できなければ本当に「読んだ」ことにはならないのです。言葉で書かれていないことを「行間を読む」と言いますが、外国語で書かれた文章の行間を読むことはなかなかむずかしいものです。本章では、行間を読むためのヒントとなる表現のパターンを学習します。

Reading with Purpose and Meaning

Drawing conclusions refers to information that is implied or inferred. This means that the information is never clearly stated.

imply 暗示する、ほのめかす
infer （結論を）ほのめかす、（見聞きしたことから）推論する

5　Writers often tell you more than they say directly. They give you hints or clues that help you "read between the lines." Using these clues to give you a deeper understanding of your reading is called **inferring**. When you **infer**, you go beyond the surface
10　details to see other meanings that the details suggest or **imply** (not stated). When the meanings of words are not stated clearly in the context of the text, they may be **implied**—that is, suggested or hinted at. When meanings are implied, you may **infer** them.

15　**Inference** is just a big word that means a **conclusion**

Chapter 18

or **judgment**. If you infer that something has happened, you do not see, hear, feel, smell, or taste the actual event. But from what you know, it makes sense to think that it has happened. Suppose you are sitting in a car at a red light. You hear screeching tires, then a loud crash and breaking glass. You see nothing, but you infer that there has been a car accident. We all know the sounds of screeching tires and a crash. We know that these sounds almost always mean a car accident. But there could be some other reason, and therefore another explanation, for the sounds. Perhaps it was not an accident involving two moving vehicles. Maybe an angry driver rammed a parked car. Making inferences means choosing the most likely explanation from the facts at hand.

There are several ways to help you draw conclusions from what an author may be implying. The following are descriptions of the various ways to help you in reaching a conclusion.

ram ～を激しくぶつける；激突する、突っ込む

General Sense

The meaning of a word may be implied by the general sense of its context, as the meaning of the word *incarcerated* is implied in the following sentence:

> *Murderers are usually **incarcerated** for longer periods of time than robbers.*

You may infer the meaning of *incarcerated* by answering the question "What usually happens to those found guilty of murder or robbery?" Use the lines below to write down what you have inferred as the meaning of the word *incarcerated*.

Antonyms and Contrasts

When the meaning of a word is not implied by the general sense of its context or by examples, it may be implied by an antonym or by a contrasting thought in a context. **Antonyms** are words that have opposite meanings, such as *happy* and *sad*. For instance,

*Ben is fearless, but his brother is **timorous**.*

You may infer the meaning of *timorous* by answering the question "If Ben is fearless and Jim is very different from Ben with regard to fear, then what word describes Jim?" Write your answer on the following line.

A **contrast** in the following sentence implies the meaning of *credence:*

*Dad gave **credence** to my story, but Mom's reaction was one of total disbelief.*

You may infer the meaning of *credence* by answering the question "If Mom's reaction was disbelief and Dad's reaction was very different from Mom's, what was Dad's reaction?

Chapter 18

Be Careful of the Meaning You Infer!

When a sentence contains an unfamiliar word, it is sometimes possible to infer the general meaning of the sentence without inferring the exact meaning of
5 the unknown word. For instance:

> *When we invite the Paulsons for dinner, they never invite us to their home for a meal; however, when we have the Browns to dinner, they always* **reciprocate**.

10 In reading this sentence some students infer that the Browns are more desirable dinner guests than the Paulsons without inferring the exact meaning of *reciprocate*. Other students conclude that the Browns differ from the Paulsons in that they do something in
15 return when they are invited for dinner; these students conclude correctly that *reciprocate* means "to do something in return."

In drawing conclusions (making inferences), you are really getting at the ultimate meaning of things—
20 what is important, why it is important, how one event influences another, how one happening leads to another.

Fact or Opinion?

Because writers don't always say things directly,
25 sometimes it is difficult to figure out what a writer really means or what he or she is really trying to say. You need to learn to "read between the lines"—to take the information the writer gives you and figure

things out for yourself.

You will also need to learn to distinguish between **fact** and **opinion**. It's important to be able to interpret what the writer is saying so you can form opinions of your own. As you read an author's views, you should ask yourself if the author is presenting you with an established **fact** or with a personal **opinion**.

The key difference between facts and opinions is that facts can be verified, or checked for accuracy, by anyone. Opinions cannot be checked for accuracy by some outside source. Opinions are what someone personally thinks or how he/she feels about an issue.

Defining a Fact

Facts are objective, concrete bits of information. They can be found in official government and legal records, and in the physical sciences. Facts can be found in reference books, such as encyclopedias and atlases, textbooks, and related publications. Since anyone can look up facts, facts are generally not the subject of arguments. However, not all facts are complete.

To sum up, facts:

- can be verified in reference books, official records, and so forth.
- are expressed in concrete language or specific numbers.
- once verified, are generally agreed upon by people.

encyclopedia 百科事典

Chapter 18

Determining an Opinion

An opinion is a belief that someone holds without complete proof or positive knowledge that it is correct. Opinions are often expressed as comparisons
5 (more, strongest, less, most, least efficient, but):

*The painter Pablo Picasso was far **more** innovative than any of his contemporaries.*

Opinions are often expressed by adjectives (brilliant, vindictive, fair, trustworthy):

vindictive 報復的な

10 *Ronald Reagan was a **convincing** speaker when he read a prepared address but was not **effective** at press conferences.*

Opinions often involve evaluations:

*The **excellence** of her science project was a **model**
15 for other students.*

Opinions are often introduced by verbs and adverbs that suggest some doubt in the writer's mind:

*It **appears** she was confused.*
*She **seems** to have the qualifications for the posi-
20 tion.*
*They **probably** used dirty tricks to win.*

Become an alert and critical reader. Understand the differences between facts and opinions, and interpret and apply both into your critical thinking.

Chapter 18

Exercise

Answer true or false.

1. What does this sentence mean?
   Drawing conclusions refers to information that is implied or inferred.
2. How do writers help you "read between the lines"?
3. What is *inferring* and how do you do it?
4. What happens when we *imply* something?
5. What happens when you *infer* that something has happened?
6. What is the key difference between *facts* and *opinions*?

Chapter 19
Reading and Remembering!

小説などは読んで楽しめばそれで十分かもしれませんが、学校の課題であれば、内容の理解を試すテストが課されることもありますから、読んで終わりというわけにはいきません。本章では、読んだものを効果的に記憶に定着させる方法を学びます。読前・読中・読後それぞれの段階でできることがあります。教科書を読む時に役立つヒントも書かれていますから、次回のテスト対策としてぜひ活用してみてください。

In this chapter, I present you with a system for a better way of reading a textbook and remembering more about what you have read. Try it and prove to yourself that it does work.

How to Remember What You Read

What you do **before** and **after** you read is as important as the reading itself. Learning is an **active** process that requires attention and energy.

1. Survey

- Look over a chapter for a few minutes before studying it in depth.
- Read the title and introductory paragraph(s). Often the introduction to the chapter supplies background for recognizing the purpose of the chapter.
- Read headings, subheadings, and italicized words. Go through the chapter heading by heading; these will form a **topical** (of current interest) outline.

Chapter 19

- Read the summary at the end of the chapter.
- Reread it to see which ideas the author repeats for special importance or what general conclusions he or she comes to.

2. Before reading
- Use the chapter survey to set in motion your prior knowledge of the subject.
- Recall what you already know about the subject by trying to expect the chapter's main points.
- Use the chapter survey to predict the principal thought patterns.
- Use surveying to predict which portions or sections of the chapter will be most difficult or challenging.

3. While reading
- Use the survey as a guide to what is important to learn.
- Highlight, mark or underline key information mentioned in the survey.

4. After reading
- Use the survey to check the success of your reading.
- Test your ability to recall the key information.
- Review immediately any material you were unable to recall.

5. Question
- Put together questions before you read the material.
- Turn each heading and subtitle into a question. (Who? What? When? Where? Why? How?). You

set 〜 in motion　〜を作動させる、働かせる

should be able to answer these questions when you finish reading and studying the paragraph, section, or chapter.

6. Read

Read the material.
- Read only the material covered under one heading or subheading at a time, and
- Look for the answers to your questions.
- Read ideas, not just words. Take only the least amount notes while reading.
- Read with the goal of getting answers, noting supporting details, and remembering.

7. Recite

Do "question-read-recite" for each subheading.
- Answer the questions that you raised before you began to read.
- Tell yourself the major concept(s) of the section. Put the ideas into your own words.

If you simply read a textbook chapter, you will probably remember less than one third of what you read by the following week. In two months, you will remember about 14% of the material, hardly enough to do well on a test.

In order to move a greater part of the material you read from your short-term to long-term memory, you must do something active with the information to help "attach" it to your memory. If you take time after reading each section of the chapter to recite the information, you will make sure that more of it goes into

recite 暗唱する

long-term memory. If you recite, you are likely to remember 80% of what you read after a week and 70% after two months.

8. Record

After having read a section and thought about on what you have read and questioned yourself about the material, you are ready to take notes. Taking notes at this point in time will almost ensure that you are noting the important parts of the section. Go back over the paragraphs and highlight or underline only the main ideas and supporting details with no more than 10–15% of the page highlighted.

9. Review

- Look over your notes and the headings and subheadings in the text.
- Recall supporting details under each main point.
- Predict test questions based on these main points, especially questions that would fall into the important and imaginative levels of reading comprehension.
- Try true/false and completion-type questions from details.

How to Read a Textbook
Organizational Patterns of Paragraphs

Perhaps one of the best ways to improve your reading ability is to learn to read paragraphs skillfully. Many experts believe the paragraph, not the sentence, is the basic unit of thought in a selection.

It is important to see the author's viewpoint by dis-

Chapter 19

covering how the message is being sent. Every writer has a purpose for writing and some plan of action for getting a message across. This plan of action is the order in which the material will be presented in the text. This order, called **a pattern of organization**, should be present in writing from the smallest to the largest unit of writing.

Anticipating the order in which the material will be presented helps you to see how the parts fit into the whole. For example, if the selection begins by indicating that there are four important components of management, you are alert to look for four key phrases to mark and remember. Likewise if a comparison is suggested, you want to note the points that are compared. For material that shows cause and effect, you need to anticipate the connection and note the relationship.

The importance of these patterns is that they signal how the facts will be presented.

In textbooks, the number of details can be overpowering. The mind responds to logical patterns; relating the small parts to the whole makes easier the difficulty of the material and makes remembering easier.

overpowering 圧倒するような

Although key **signal words** help in identifying the particular type of pattern, a single paragraph can be a mixture of different patterns.

The following six examples are the patterns of organization that are most frequently found in textbooks.

1. **Simple Listing**—Items are randomly listed in a series of supporting facts or details. These supporting elements are of identical value, and the order in which they are presented is of no importance.

   Signal words often used for simple listing are:
   - in addition
   - also
   - another
   - several
   - for example
   - a number of

2. **Description**—Description is like listing; the characters that make up a description are no more than a simple listing of details.

3. **Definition**—Frequently in textbook reading an entire paragraph is devoted to defining a complex term or idea. The idea is initially defined and then further expanded with examples and restatements.

   Signal words often used for definition are:
   - is defined as
   - is called
   - means
   - refers to
   - is described as
   - term
   - concept

4. **Chronological (Time) Order or Sequence**—Items are listed in the order in which they occurred or in a specifically planned order in which they

devote 捧げる、充てる、投入する

must develop. In this case, the order is important and changing it would change the meaning.

Signal words often used for chronological order or sequence are:

> first, second, third
> until
> before, after
> at last
> when
> next
> later

5. **Comparison/Contrast**—Items are related by the comparisons (similarities) that are made or by the contrasts (differences) that are presented.

Signal words often used for comparison/contrast are:

> similar, different
> bigger than, smaller than
> on the other hand
> in the same way
> but
> parallels
> however

6. **Cause and Effect**—In this pattern, one item is shown as having produced another element. An event (effect) is said to have happened because of some situation or circumstance (cause). The cause (the action) stimulates the event, or effect (the outcome).

Signal words often used for cause and effect are:

> for this reason

Chapter 19

hence
consequently
because
on that account

Exercise

Answer true or false.

1. Why should you look over a chapter before studying it in depth?
2. Why is what you do before and after you read important?
3. What should you do while reading?
4. Why is learning to read paragraphs one of the best ways to improve your reading ability?
5. What are the 6 patterns of organization?

Chapter 20
Concentrating and Remembering

前章では読んだ内容を記憶に定着させるための方法を見てきましたが、記憶に関してはもう1つ重要な要素があります。それはあなた自身の「集中力」です。集中して読んだ内容はより深く、強く記憶に定着します。では、集中力を高め、維持するためにはどうしたらよいのでしょうか。本章では、集中力を強化するための心理的なスキルを学びます。

Better Concentration

Any attempt on your part to remember more of what you read involves your ability to concentrate on the material you are reading. Intense concentration increases the time you spend attending to the task, an important element in reading. Students who are restless in their actions often find it difficult to concentrate for any length of time. Likewise, students who are passive in their approach to learning—those who are not actively engaged and thinking about what they are reading—often fail to get involved with the material enough to concentrate for long periods of time. Here are some ways to improve your concentration:

- **Improve your attitude**—Some subjects you will encounter in university may not be of high interest to you. Not only that, some subjects may not seem appropriate to your field of study. You must maintain a positive attitude however and realize there is a job to be done! To get your degree, you must pass all these courses, not just the ones you like.

- **Attend to the task**—Concentration is a must for successful reading. Yet many distractions may be encountered which lessen your ability to stick to the task and concentrate for long periods of time. A good idea is to keep a "distraction list" of times you were interrupted from concentrating on your reading. The list may include items such as: a) type of book being read; b) number of minutes reading before distraction; c) type of distraction; d) amount of time taken by the distraction; and e) a goal to improve. Concentration is improved if you study when you are the most alert, least tired and in good physical condition. During your scheduled breaks, get up from your desk and walk around or do something physical for about 10 minutes.

  distraction 気を散らすこと・物
  lessen 減少させる（する）

- **Establish a purpose**—If you first determine a purpose for reading, you then have a reason for thinking as well as for completing the reading assignment. Purpose helps focus your attention and improve your concentration. Write out some questions that relate to the subject matter you are about to read. For instance, what specifically do you want to know or need to know about this subject? By pre-selecting questions to answer, you become an active member in the learning/reading process.

- **Eliminate emotional stress**—Rid yourself of restless and evasion behavior due to overwhelming daily stress by keeping a "blame list." This is a list

  evasion 回避すること、言い逃れ

of all the people, situations, circumstances, etc. that you blame for your evasion behavior. Your blame list can be a benefit in getting you to face your problems squarely. If you find yourself in the middle of a brief depression or emotional upheaval, do something physical or any activity that is not mind taxing.

Remember to maintain a positive attitude, avoid negative people and influences, stay active in the learning process without being hyperactive about it, keep a list of distractions to help eliminate restless behavior, choose carefully your place and time to study, and try physical activity to burn off stress and to maintain an alert mind.

Remembering!
A push from short-term to long-term memory

To transfer information from short-term to long-term (permanent) memory, the brain has to perform several functions. The brain by nature is a choosy organ, committing to permanent memory only those items it thinks are absolutely necessary to retain. You must determine what is important and what is just feathers. If the information is important and needs to be stored, you must perform a necessary operation to insure transfer into permanent memory. This process is called **recitation** or **verbalization**. You help to transfer the information through the recitation process by repeating the information over and over again, or by shortening the information in your own words. This process of reciting important information allows the brain to permanently store the information. Recitation is the best way to commit large amounts of information to long-term memory.

Organize Information

Classifying large amounts of information into categories can help you remember information more correctly and recover information faster. For instance, suppose you had to learn the following concepts for a business class:

tools, labor, trees, wildlife, human resources, minerals, machinery, capital resources, factories, tractors, water, power plants, manpower, natural resource, typewriters

These concepts would be difficult to learn and remember if you were merely trying to memorize the individual terms. If you classify these terms into major categories, you will place a value on the terms and give them meaning. These individual terms could be held in short-term memory long enough for you to push them into long-term memory by using the recitation process. For example:

Natural Resources	Capital Resources	Human Resources
minerals	tools	labor
water	machinery	manpower
trees	power plants	
wildlife	factories	
	tractors	
	typewriters	

If you stop your reading often to review and categorize, it will be easier to speak the information at the end of the reading, thereby, improving your long-term memory.

Mnemonic Devices

Mnemonic aids (from the Greek word meaning "to bring to mind") are specific memory improving techniques which can be useful in learning huge amounts of seemingly unrelated information. Mnemonic devices are best suitable for remembering facts and least helpful in the interpretation of facts or in relating learned material to your life situations.

Some mnemonic examples are:

> rhymes
> acronyms
> catch phrases
> association by image
> peg words

Motivation

You are your own best motivator. Your motivation must come from within yourself. Others may try to encourage you, but you are the only one who can accomplish what you desire. You must convince yourself—you can!

rhyme 押韻
acronym 頭字語

peg word ペグワード法

motivation やる気、動機づけ

Chapter 20

Exercise

Answer true or false.

1. What are some of the ways to improve your concentration?
2. What is the essential operation to insure transfer of information into permanent memory?
3. What is this process called?
4. What are *mnemonic devices* and what do they do?
5. Where does the word mnemonic come from?

Chapter 21
English Spelling Rules

本書最後の2章は英語のスペリングのルールを学びます。正しいスペリングで書くことができなければ、その単語は覚えたことにはなりません。そうです、「語彙力アップの秘密」その5は、このスペリングに関する知識です。接頭辞を加える時はスペリングの変化は起きませんので、気をつけなければいけないのは接尾辞を加える時です。第10章でも少し触れましたが、ここで改めて接尾辞を加える時のスペリングのルールをおさらいしておきましょう。

Here Is Secret #5

Knowing proper spelling is very important for a number of reasons. First of all, when words cannot be spoken from our mouths we can write them down. If these words are not spelled properly, then that message is compromised. Since communicating in writing is very important in many jobs, it is important to know some very significant grammar rules. Second, many use writing to write down their ideas. If proper grammar isn't used, then those who like to write in diaries and journals would not understand what they wrote when reading it years down the road. So not only is writing important when communicating with others, it is also important when communicating with ourselves. Below are rules regarding the addition of prefixes and suffixes to words.

compromise 危うくする、(評判・信用などを)落とす

journal 日記・日誌

Chapter 21
Adding Prefixes and Suffixes

Prefixes

Prefixes are those additions that usually do not change the spelling of the word. The prefix is attached to the word despite any consonant duplications, accents, or **syllabication** (to divide into syllables). Examples are:

unavailable: The prefix is the *un-* and it is easy to see that the remainder of the word, *available*, does not change.

misspell: Ridiculously, this word is the most misspelled word. A great way to remember how to spell *misspell* is that *mis-* is the prefix and *spell* is the main word. The spelling of the main word does not change at all, but it is amazing how often this word is not spelled correctly.

duplication 重複、複製

ridiculously おかしなことに、ばかげた話だが

Suffixes

When adding a suffix, the main part of the word usually changes the spelling of the word, but sometimes there are exceptions. Take the word *treatment*, for instance. *-ment* is the suffix of the word and *treat* is the original word. Simply add the *-ment* to *treat* and you have *treatment* without any spelling changes.

For those words that have a short vowel sound and end with a single consonant, the consonant is doubled when adding on a suffix that starts with a vowel. These suffixes can be *-ed, -ing,* or *-er*. Some examples:

biggest: big is the main word that has a short vowel sound and ends in a single consonant. As a result, we add another *g* and then the *-est* since it starts with a vowel.

There are exceptions, though. There are some words that end in *-r, -x, -w* or *-y* and don't require doubling. Such a word is *blowing*. The suffix is *-ing*, but because the single consonant is a *-w*, there is no need for doubling.

If there are two consonants at the end of your main word, or two vowels and a consonant, the consonant doesn't need to be doubled. An example is the word *keeper*. The suffix *-er* can be added on without doubling the consonant. Another thing to keep in mind is that when a suffix is added that begins with a vowel and the main words ends with a silent *e*, that silent *e* should be dropped like it is in the words: *price → pricing* and *surprise → surprising*. However, if the suffix used begins with a consonant, the silent *e* should be kept such as in the words: *like → likeness* and *advance → advancement*.

It is also necessary to drop the final *-y* in the main word when adding a suffix if the *-y* has a consonant before it. The word *worry* becomes *worried* and *supply* becomes *supplies*. But this rule does not apply to words ending in *-y* in which the *-ing* suffix is added. Examples are: *cry → crying* and *obey → obeyed/obeying*.

It is important to know the rules regarding prefixes

and suffixes when learning English. It is easy to see that there is more involved with adding a suffix than a prefix, but with practice suffixes can be added on without even thinking about them. These rules are vital for effective communication, so knowing the rules is very important.

vital	不可欠な、きわめて重要な

Basic Spelling Rules
1. The Present Progressive Tense

a) Add *-ing* to the base form of the verb.

read → reading
stand → standing
jump w → jumping

b) If a verb ends in a silent *e*, drop the final *e* and add *-ing*.

leave → leaving
take → taking
receive → receiving

c) In a one-syllable word, if the last three letters are consonant-vowel-consonant combination (CVC), double the last consonant before adding *-ing*.

sit → sitting
run → running
hop → hopping

*However, do not double the last consonant in word that end in *-w*, *-x*, or *-y*.

sew → sewing
fix → fixing
enjoy → enjoying

d) In words of two or more syllables that end in a consonant-vowel-consonant combination, double the last consonant only if the last syllable is stressed.

   admit → admitting

   regret → regretting

e) If a verb ends in *-ie*, change the *ie* to *y* before adding *-ing*.

   die → dying

2. The Simple Present Tense

a) Add *-s* for most verbs.

   work → works

   buy → buys

   ride → rides

   return → returns

b) Add *-es* for words that end in *-ch*, *-s* , *-sh*, *-x*, or *-z*.

   watch → watches

   pass → passes

   rush → rushes

   relax → relaxes

   buzz → buzzes

c) Change the *y* to *i* and add *-es* when the base form ends in a consonant + *y*.

   study → studies

   hurry → hurries

   dry → dries

   *Do not change the *y* when the base form ends

in a vowel + *y*. Add *-s*.
> *play → plays*
> *enjoy → enjoys*

d) A few verbs have irregular forms.
> *be → is*
> *do → does*
> *go → goes*
> *have → has*

3. Simple Past Tense of Regular Verbs

a) If the verb ends in a consonant, add *-ed*.
> *return → returned*
> *help → helped*
> *cook → cooked*

b) If the verb ends in *-e*, add *-d*.
> *live → lived*
> *create → created*
> *die → died*

c) In one-syllable words, if the verb ends in a consonant-vowel-consonant combination (CVC), double the last consonant and add *-ed*.
> *hop → hopped*
> *rub → rubbed*

*However, do not double one-syllable words ending in *-w*, *-x*, or *-y*.
> *bow → bowed*
> *play → played*
> *mix → mixed*

d) In words of two or more syllables that end in consonant-vowel-consonant combination, double the last consonant only if the last syllable is stressed.

prefer → *preferred* (The last syllable is stressed)
visit → *visited* (The last syllable isn't stressed)

e) If the verb ends in a consonant + *y*, change the *y* to *i* and add *-ed*.
worry → *worried*
annoy → *annoyed*

f) If the verb ends in a vowel + *y*, add *-ed*. (Do not change the *y* to *i*.)
play → *played*
annoy → *annoyed*
Exception: *pay* → *paid*
lay → *laid*
say → *said*

4. The Comparative (-er) & Superlative (-est) Adjectives

a) Add *-er* to one-syllable adjectives to form the comparative. Add *-est* to one-syllable adjectives to form the superlative.
cheap → *cheaper* → *cheapest*
bright → *brighter* → *brightest*

b) If the adjective ends in *-e*, add *-r* or *-st*.
nice → *nicer* → *nicest*

c) If the adjective ends in a consonant + *y*, change to *y* to *i* before you add *-er* or *-est*.
   pretty → prettier → prettiest
   Exception: *shy → shyer → shyest*

d) If the adjective ends in a consonant-vowel-consonant combination (CVC), double the final consonant before adding -er or -est.
   big → bigger → biggest

   *However, do not double the consonant in words ending in *-w*, or *-y*.
   slow → slower → slowest
   coy → coyer → coyest   coy 遠慮がちな

5. Adverbs

a) Add *-ly* to the corresponding adjectives.
   nice → nicely
   quiet → quietly
   quick → quickly
   beautiful → beautifully

b) If the adjective ends in consonant + *y*, change the *y* to *i* before adding *-ly*.
   easy → easily

c) If the adjective ends in *-le*, drop the *e* and add *y*.
   possible → possibly

   *However, do not drop the *e* for other adjectives ending in *-e*.
   extreme → extremely

Chapter 21

Exception: *true → truly*

d) If the adjective ends in *-ic*, add *-ally*.
   basic → basically
   fantastic → fantastically
   terrific → terrifically

Exercise

Answer true or false.

1. What should be done when adding a suffix, for those words that have a short vowel sound and end with a single consonant?
2. What should be done if there are two consonants at the end of your main word, or two vowels and a consonant?
3. What should be done when a suffix is added that begins with a vowel and the main words ends with a silent *e*?
4. What should be done however, if the suffix used begins with a consonant?
5. When is it necessary to drop the final *y* in the main word?

Chapter 22
Exceptions to the Rules

言語には例外がつきものです。前章で見てきた接尾辞を加える時のスペリングのルールにも、いくつかの例外があります。本章では、ルールと例外を対比させる形で説明していきます。英語のスペリングは一見、発音と対応していないように見えますが、一定のルールはあります。しかし、例外はとても多く、ネイティブスピーカーでさえ覚えるのに苦労しています。本章後半では、そのような"不規則なスペリング"の単語を見ていきます。

The basic spelling rules presented in the previous chapter apply to the spelling of thousands of words. However, commonly used words that are exceptions to these rules are the point of this chapter.

RULE: When a word ends in a single consonant preceded by a single vowel and the word is one syllable or accented on the last syllable, then double the final consonant when adding a vowel suffix.

beg → begged/begging
occur → occurred/occurring
(Also remember that it is *transferred* and *transferring* although the accent is on the first syllable.)

Exceptions: Words ending in -w or -x
flow → flowed/flowing
fix → fixed/fixing

RULE: When adding a vowel suffix to a word ending in *-e*, the *-e* is dropped.

> *care* → *cared/caring*
> *desire* → *desired/desiring/desirable*

Exceptions: To prevent confusion with other words or for pronunciation purposes, the following words are exceptions.

> *acre* → *acreage*
> *canoe* → *canoeing*
> *dye* → *dyeing* (to change color)
> *mile* → *mileage*
> *singe* → *singeing* (to burn slightly)
> (Also remember that for words ending in *-ce* or *-ge*, the *-e* is kept if the vowel suffix begins with *-a* or *-o*.)

RULE: Adding a consonant suffix does not change the spelling of a word.

> *pain + ful* → *painful*
> *rapid + ly* → *rapidly*
> *complete + ly* → *completely*

Exceptions:

> *acknowledge + ment* → *acknowledgment*
> *argue + ment* → *argument*
> *judge + ment* → *judgment*
> *nine + th* → *ninth*
> *true + ly* → *truly*

RULE: If a word ends in *-y* preceded by a consonant, change the *y* to *i*, then add the suffix.

> *beauty + ful* → *beautiful*
> *try + ed* → *tried*

Exceptions:
>*dry + ness → dryness*
>*shy + ness → shyness*
>*sly + ness → slyness*

(Also remember that the *y* is kept when adding *-ing*.)

RULE: If a word ends in *-y* preceded by a vowel, then the *y* is kept when a suffix is added.
>*annoy → annoyed/annoying*
>*journey → journeyed/journeying*

Exceptions:
>*day + ly   daily*

RULE: A prefix does not change the spelling of a word.
>*dis + able → disable*
>*un + necessary → unnecessary*

Exceptions: none

RULE: When two words are joined to form a compound word, leave out no letters.
>*room + mate → roommate*
>*book + keeper → bookkeeper*

Exceptions:
>*past + time → pastime*
>*where + ever → wherever*

Impediments to Spelling

The nature of the English language contributes to

spelling difficulties in several ways. These difficulties are explored in detail, through examples, on the pages that follow.

As you review these pages, you will note that a speller must remember several factors when learning to spell new words. For example, the sound of long *a* (|ā|) can be written in at least eighteen ways. How many students realize that the |ā| is spelled *et* in words of French origin, such as *chalet* and *bouquet*? Other unique factors that provide problems for spellers are also addressed. After studying these pages, you will also conclude that a strong visual memory contributes significantly to spelling success.

chalet　シャレー（アルプス地方の山小屋）

Keep in mind these two considerations when making decisions about spelling words to be studied:

- Students should only study high-use words that are part of their reading and listening vocabularies.
- Meanings of words should already be known before formal spelling is undertaken.

undertake　着手する

Irregular Spellings

Some words are not spelled as they sound and present problems even for native speakers. For example, the word *said* might be spelled as *sed* according to its pronunciation. The sound of short *e* is usually spelled with *e* as in *led* and *fed* and the use of *ai* is an irregular spelling. The following table shows more words with irregular spellings.

Table 22–1 Words with Irregular Spellings

Word	Pronunciation	Word	Pronunciation
ache	ayk	lawyer	LAW yur
acre	AY kur	light	lyt
again	uh GEN	machine	muh SHEEN
answer	AN sur	mother	MUHTH ur
antique	an TEEK	nymph	NIHMf
any	EN ee	ocean	OH shun
because	bih KAWZ	of	uhv
become	bih KUHM	often	AW fun
been	bihn	once	Wuhns
bologna	buh LOH nee	only	OHN lee
bridge	brihj	people	PEE pul
castle	KAS ul	phantom	FAN tum
catch	kach	pharaoh	FAY roh
chamois	SHAM ee	phrase	frayz
chaos	KAY as	physical	FIHZ ih kul
circuit	SUR kiht	please	pleez
climb	klym	quote	kwoht
color	KUHL ur	recede	ree SEED
comfortable	KUHM fur tuh bul	rhyme	rym
could	cud	rough	ruhf
country	KUHN tree	said	sed
cycle	SYE kul	seize	seez
debut	day BYOO	should	shud
depot	DEE poh	straight	strayt
do	doo	sure	shur
does	duhz	they	thay
door	dor	thought	thawttuh
dumb	duhm	today	tuh DAY
earth	urth	trough	trawf
enough	ih NUHF	Tuesday	TUZ day

eye	ahy	unique	yoo NEEK
father	FAH thur	vegetable	VEJ tuh bul
few	fyoo	victuals	VIHT lz
find	fynd	was	wuhz
friends	frendz	water	WAW tur
from	fruhm	Wednesday	WENZ day
height	hyt	were	wur
indict	ihn DYT	what	hwaht
journey	JUR nee	who	hoo
knee	nee	young	yuhng

Spelling of Sounds at the Beginning of Words

Before you look up a word in a dictionary, you must have some idea how to spell it. This is sometimes difficult, because the same sound may be spelled in many different ways. Below is a simplified table of some of the common alternate ways that sounds can be spelled at the beginning of words.

Table 22–2 Spellings of Consonant Sounds	
Consonant Sounds	**Common Alternate Spellings**
b, d, l, m, p, sh, t, th, v, and w	Usually spelled the way they sound
f as in face	ph (phone)
g as in gas	gh (ghost), gu (guard)
h as in hole	wh (who)
j as in join	g followed by e, i, or y: (gentle, gin, gym)
k as in kitten	c (coin), ch (chord), qu (queen)
n as in nice	kn (know), gn (gnaw), pn (pneumonia)
r as in rice	rh (rhino), wr (write)
s as in save	c or sc followed by e, i, or y (cent, scent, science)
sk as in skin	sc (score), sch (school)
ch as in child	c (cello)

Chapter 22

Table 22–3 Spellings of Vowel Sounds	
Vowel Sounds	**Common Alternate Spellings**
a as in able	ai (aim)
a as in at	a (at)
a as in area	ai (air), e (ere)
a as in father	a (argument)
e as in equal	ea (eat), ee (eel), ei (either)
e as in lend	e (end)
er as in her	er (ermine), ear (earth), ur (urge)
i as in ice	ei (either)
i as in hit	i (it), e (electric)
o as in open	oa (oats), ow (owe)
o as in hot	o (odd)
o as in often	aw (awful), oa (oar), a (all), au (auto), ou (ought)
ou as in out	ow (owl)
u as in up	o (oven)
schwa*	a, e, i, o, u

*unstressed vowel sound that begins *about, event, oblige, upon,* etc.

Exercise

Answer true or false.

1. When should you double the final consonant when adding a vowel suffix?
2. What words are the exceptions to the above rule?
3. What should be done when adding a vowel suffix to a word ending in *-e*?
4. What should be done if a word ends in *-y* preceded by a consonant?
5. What should you do when two words are joined to form a compound word?

Chapter 23
Conclusion

In conclusion, I would like to clarify that the items I called "secrets" are really not secrets. They are things that all native speakers have learned from the cradle so to speak, which a lot of native speakers take for granted. Foreign students have not had this opportunity or knowledge to take advantage of, which creates problems for them in their study of English.

The students who study and learn the meanings of prefixes, word roots and suffixes and how to use them, will become better readers. They will become more confident of their English abilities. They will score higher on the English tests they take—and are bound to become better speakers of the language. This is something I firmly believe!

cradle　ゆりかご

take 〜 for granted　〜を当たり前だと思う

be bound to do　（当然）〜することとなる、しなければならない

資料提供／編集協力
Cuesta College Academic Support in San Luis Obispo, California, USA.

リーディングに効く
語彙力アップの秘密

● 2009年11月1日初版発行 ●

● 著者 ●

Gabriel David Munoz ＋ 水嶋いづみ

© Gabriel David Munoz, Izumi Mizushima, 2009

● 発行者 ●

関戸 雅男

● 発行所 ●

株式会社 研究社

〒102-8152 東京都千代田区富士見 2-11-3
電話 営業 03-3288-7777（代）
    編集 03-3288-7711（代）
振替 00150-9-26710
http://www.kenkyusha.co.jp/

● 印刷所 ●

研究社印刷株式会社

● 装丁・本文レイアウト ●

寺澤 彰二

ISBN978-4-327-42180-9 C1082 Printed in Japan

KENKYUSHA
〈検印省略〉